*Islamic Identity
and the
Struggle
for Justice*

Islamic Identity and the Struggle for Justice

Edited by
Nimat Hafez Barazangi
M. Raquibuz Zaman
Omar Afzal

University Press of Florida
Gainesville Tallahassee Tampa Boca Raton
Pensacola Orlando Miami Jacksonville

Copyright 1996
by the Board of Regents
of the State of Florida

Printed in the
United States of America
on acid-free paper
All rights reserved

Library of Congress Cataloging-in-Publication Data

Islamic Identity and the struggle for justice/edited
by Nimat Hafez Barazangi,
M. Raquibuz Zaman, Omar Afzal.
p. cm.
Includes bibliographical references and index.
ISBN 0-8130-1862-5 (alk. paper)
1. Islam and justice. I. Barazangi, Nimat Hafez,
1943–
II. Zaman, M. Raquibuz. III. Afzal, Omar.
BP173.43.I86 1996
297'.1978—dc20 95-23907

The University Press of Florida is the scholarly
publishing agency for the State University System
of Florida, comprised of Florida A & M University,
Florida Atlantic University, Florida International
University, Florida State University, University of
Central Florida, University of Florida, University of
North Florida, University of South Florida, and
University of West Florida.

University Press of Florida
15 Northwest 15th Street
Gainesville, FL 32611

In memory of
Lois Lamya' Ibsen
and
Isma'il Raji al Faruqi

Contents

Preface ix
Introduction 1

Part One
Justice: The Ideals

Chapter 1. Islam's Origin and Ideals
Fazlur Rahman 11

Chapter 2. The Islamic Concept of Justice
Mahmoud Ayoub 19

Chapter 3. Comparative View of Justice
I. The Concept of Justice in Judaism
Laurence Edwards 27
II. A Christian Understanding of Justice:
Reflections for an Interfaith Discussion
Byron Lee Haines 30
III. Justice in Islam, Judaism, and
Christianity: A Comparison
Charles Adams 38

Connecting the Ideals to Practice
*Nimat Hafez Barazangi, M. Raquibuz Zaman,
and Omar Afzal* 41

Part Two
Justice: The Reality

Chapter 4. Economic Justice in Islam,
Ideals and Reality:
The Cases of Malaysia, Pakistan,
and Saudi Arabia
M. Raquibuz Zaman 47

Chapter 5. The Islamic Call:
Social Justice and Political Realism
Tamara Sonn 64

Chapter 6. Vicegerency and
Gender Justice in Islam
Nimat Hafez Barazangi 77

Chapter 7. The Nuclear Option
and International Justice:
Islamic Perspectives
Ali A. Mazrui 95

Contributors 117
Index 120

بسم الله الرحمن الرحيم

Bismi Allah Al Rahman Al Rahim

Preface

The youngest of the three monotheistic religions in the world, Islam is now in its fifteenth century of existence. Its adherents—estimated to be more than a billion people, or about one-fifth of humanity—are scattered all over the globe, with major concentrations in Asia and Africa. Today, more than fifty Muslim countries are struggling to emerge from several centuries of sociopolitical and economic hibernation. They often find themselves misunderstood, stigmatized, and marginalized by the non-Islamic world, especially the technologically modern nations of the West. Muslims are finding that the Western media tend to interpret all their actions and aspirations in religious terms despite the fact that their sociopolitical and economic structures are primarily the result of imperial Westernized systems. A secular, sociopolitical context seems to be reserved for the West even though religious assumptions underlie almost every action in those countries. Although there is no separation between religion and the state in Islam, very few media and academic professionals in the West acknowledge that most modern Muslim states neither operate according to the teachings of Islam nor represent the people they govern. Moreover, few groups or individuals question the validity of secularism and the separation of religion and state in the functions of the Western "liberal" countries.

Although the Quran and the teachings of the Prophet Muhammad (peace be upon him [PBUH]) have given Muslims a general understanding of Judaism and Christianity, Jews and Christians usually have little, if any, knowledge about Islam. Perhaps this lack of knowledge, combined with a history of religious warfare between the Christians and the Muslims, has reinforced the conflict and mistrust shared by Muslims and the non-Muslim West. Misunderstandings have increased with the West's creation of Israel, which displaced millions of people; the Iranian Revolution and the ensuing Gulf conflicts; and the genocide of Bosnian and Chechnyan Muslims.

In this book we hope to foster a better understanding among the followers of the three monotheistic revealed religions, particularly about religious teachings and practices that concern individual and social conducts of behavior. We present Islam as a pedagogical system concerned with the development of Islamic identity. Before Islam was solidified in the existing juristic law and perceived as a religious tradition, it was based on the needs of communal living in a just society. In that spirit, we are seeking a dialogue between Muslims and Westerners that allows both parties to examine how their perspectives of Islam have evolved. The dialogue may also help non-Muslims in Western societies understand their own identity by relating to Muslims as partners rather than subjects of study.

Muslim scholars and lay people have long been ready to participate in a dialogue with their Western counterparts despite the persistent injustice they have faced from the West. The time has come for Western scholars and people to join this dialogue and attempt to understand Muslims instead of marginalizing them. Whether or not Westerners participate, Muslims will continue to resist injustice, mainly because Islam's first goal is to instill *'Adl* (justice). The intensity of Muslims' emphasis on identity and the potency of their resistance will depend on whether or not they are treated justly, especially by Christians and Jews of the West.

The idea for this volume emerged from a three-day symposium titled "Islam and the Struggle for Justice in the World Today," which was held at Cornell University in September 1987. Our book is based on the revised version of a number of papers that were presented and discussed at that symposium, including the writings of both Muslim and non-Muslim scholars.

Several years elapsed between our first attempt to publish the collective manuscript and the appearance of this volume, a testimony to the difficulty of publishing a nongeopolitical, Islamic view of justice. We only wish that two of our contributors, Fazlur Rahman (1919–88) and Byron Lee Haines (1928–90), were still among us to celebrate our publication. This volume, therefore, is both a tribute to Rahman and Haines and a dedication to the memory of the al Faruqis—Lois Lamya'

Ibsen (1926–86) and Ismaʻil Raji (1921–86). The year 1996 not only celebrates this work's publication but marks the tenth anniversary of the assassination of these two Islamic scholars, for whom justice is still undone.

We would like to thank the following people for their assistance. Robert L. Johnson, director of Cornell University's United Religious Work (CURW), and Philip B. Snyder, director of the university's Center for Religion, Ethics, and Social Policy (CRESP), provided encouragement and support. Gail V. Riina and Sara Hess, assistant directors at CURW and CRESP, respectively, contributed significantly to organizing the 1987 symposium. The Office of the Provost, University Lectures, the International Student Programming Board, the Africana Studies and Research Center, Near Eastern Studies, and South Asia Studies (all at Cornell) and Ithaca College cosponsored the symposium; and Mobil Oil helped to finance it. Nimat Hafez Barazangi prepared the manuscript for publication. We would like to thank Baha Abu-Laban at the University of Alberta for his comments and suggestions, and all the symposium participants for their dedication to justice and Islamic scholarship. Special thanks are also due to Patricia Darsie, Sid Doan, and Kelly Meyer for their assistance in correspondence and manuscript preparation. Without the interest and support of Walda Metcalf, associate director and editor-in-chief of the University Press of Florida, this volume would not have materialized.

Ithaca, New York   Nimat Hafez Barazangi
                                    M. Raquibuz Zaman
                                    Omar Afzal

Introduction

This book presents the religious ideals of justice and shows how such precepts are translated into the individual, social, political, and economic lives of people. We do not present an Islamic theory of justice or a full history of the Islamic conception of it, as the work of Majid Khadduri and others has already done.[1] Nevertheless, we offer some Muslim perspectives on these issues and compare them with Jewish and Christian viewpoints. Although we consider the practice of Islamic justice, we do not recount contemporary movements toward the restoration of an Islamic State. Neither do we present an apologetic, idealistic image of Islam vis-à-vis the West. Rather, we attempt to explain the concept and practice of justice in ways that avoid geopolitics and confrontations.

Our book challenges the reader to accept multiple perspectives within a unified theme. Islamic identity is organically connected to the meanings derived from the ideals. Therefore, the process of applying justice represents only one aspect of Islam, not the entire ideal or Islamic identity. Our goal is to promote a realization of the existence of diversity among Muslim countries and a reassessment of the widely held assumption that the Muslim world is monolithic. Our dual focus and the disparity between ideal and practice that has plagued the Muslim world, particularly during the last two centuries, require a serious effort in light of a renewed interest in multi- and interdisciplinary studies. Therefore, we include discussions of justice and gender equality in the social, economic, and political arenas as well as our consideration of international equality of justice.

The task of promoting a better understanding of Islam in the West is a formidable one. It is imperative, however, that we make a beginning.

Part 1 of this volume is concerned with the fields of Islamic studies and comparative study of religion. The contributions in the first three chapters underline points of convergence and divergence in the three religious traditions in terms of how justice is conceived and in the mechanics of its implementation. Though the Islamic institution of justice is as old as Muslim jurists' preoccupation with the issue of justice, the new world order requires a fresh analysis and a renewed outlook. Following the transition from ideal to practice, part 2 of this volume provides timely discussion of the reawakening identity in the Muslim world.

Chapter 1, "Islam's Origin and Ideals" by Fazlur Rahman, serves as an introduction to the socioeconomic condition and the nature of religious beliefs in Arabia in general and in Makkah (Mecca) in particular at the commencement of the prophethood of Muhammad (PBUH); the concept of God in Islam as explained by the Quranic verses; *Iman, Islam,* and *Taqwa,* the three central terms in the Quran that call for God consciousness and propel human beings to act responsibly; and the concepts of *'Adl* and *Qist,* which denote justice, equity, and fair play. What is most significant of Rahman's perspective is his explication of human integrity and justice as the goal and essence of Islamic revelation. This unique explanation brings the concept and practice of justice closer within the ideals of Islam.

Chapter 2, "The Islamic Concept of Justice" by Mahmoud Ayoub, details the Quranic terms defining justice in Islam, which he interprets as "a way of relating to one another without having anyone come up short." He links the term *al Wasat,* or the middle course, with *'Adl* or justice and explains how the *Mu'tazilites* and the *Shi'ites* made *'Adl* a primary concern of faith, indifferent to *al Wasat*. Ayoub interprets the Quranic term *Qist* as the guiding principle of social justice in its broadest sense, while *'Adl* connotes justice more in a legalistic sense. Ayoub contends that justice can be *individual,* "open only for God to know," or *public,* subject to human interpretations, or in the case of political justice espoused by various schools of Muslim political thought.

Chapters 1 and 2 provide the reader with an overview of the concepts and precepts of justice in Islam. How do those concepts and precepts compare with Judaic and Christian interpretations of justice? That question is the focus of chapter 3, which is divided into three separately authored sections.

In section 1 of chapter 3, "The Concept of Justice in Judaism," Laurence Edwards reminds us that for centuries the Jews lived as minorities without full political power and with few opportunities to practice and develop Jewish legal codes other than through interpretation and study of the legal sanctions of the Torah. He asserts that "*Midat Hadin* or God's justice is balanced by *Midat Harahamim* or God's mercy, though there is no exact formula for balancing the two." The term *Tsedeg* (righteousness) usually refers to the broad ideal of justice, while *Mishpat* (judgment) connotes the legal procedure for achieving justice. The latter is so important to the Jewish tradition that the proper functioning of law courts is part of the seven "Noachide" laws (the laws given to Noah by God after the Great Flood). The creation of legal institutions to enforce *Tsedeg* is emphasized in Torah.

Section 2 of chapter 3, "A Christian Understanding of Justice: Reflections for an Interfaith Discussion" by Byron Lee Haines, points out that there are differences of opinion among Christians about justice. In spite of this, it is possible to present an overall Christian view of justice because of major points of agreement among the diverse groups. One view of Christian justice is the law of the land as asserted by apostle Paul. Others contend that in some cases the laws of the land are counter to the divine laws, and, as such, need to be violated. They also seek guidance from the apostle Paul. The Christian beliefs of justice emanate from three sources: "commitment to God through Christ"; "in the Scripture"; and "in the tradition of the Church." The substance of justice in Christianity, according to Haines, is the concept of righteousness. God by nature is righteous, and human beings, as creatures of God, are to be righteous. But this can only be achieved "by the grace and mercy of God." The Christians believe that righteousness is in the divine revelation in God's word and "in the living word of God manifested in the person they call Jesus Christ." An integral part of the belief is the position that justice, a gift from God, cannot be separated from the human tendency to commit "sin," because this proneness to committing sin stands in the way of achieving divine justice. This can only be overcome, according to Christians, when one commits "wholly and fully to God's saving act in Christ." Haines then outlines how justice in practice has evolved into some form of dual loyalty to the state and to God in the Christian lands.

Section 3 of chapter 3, "Justice in Islam, Judaism, and Christianity: A Comparison" by Charles Adams, tries to assess how the various notions of justice expounded by the three religions have been put into practice. Except for the Jewish law that "provides for courts, lays down rules of evidence" and the like, the other two religions have not worked out adequately "the procedural side of the matter of justice." Adams argues that the Islamic notion of justice is well developed by scholars sitting and researching in their studies, far away from the courthouses and judicial decisions adjudicated by the *Qadis* (Islamic judges). Muslim rulers who promulgated their own laws to suit their own purposes rarely allowed the *Qadis* jurisdiction beyond certain limited arenas.

Adams also questions whether in Western secular states raising the question of justice "in terms of the individual and his inwardness" is possible. The Christian notion of "righteousness equals justice," implying the concept of sin and salvation from sin, fails to explain how inward righteousness is a means for achieving social justice. Adams concludes by pointing out that none of the other authors brought out the issue of reward or punishment for actions in this world now, or the religious teachings regarding the ultimate destiny awaiting an individual.

The three chapters in part 1 discuss the basic precepts of Islam and the ideals of justice in Judaism, Christianity, and Islam. A transitional essay entitled "Connecting the Ideals to Practice" precedes part 2. Part 2 is devoted to the question of justice in reality. The first three chapters in part 2 (chapters 4 through 6) deal with various aspects of the practice of justice in Muslim states and communities, and the last chapter deals with international justice as related to nuclear proliferation.

In chapter 4, "Economic Justice in Islam, Ideals and Reality: The Cases of Malaysia, Pakistan, and Saudi Arabia," M. Raquibuz Zaman examines the principal goals of Islamic economic systems and how they are to be achieved following the basic tenets advanced by Islam. He points out that while Islam allows and indeed encourages individual choice and freedom in economic endeavors, it recognizes the role of the state in providing social goods and services and in enforcing economic justice and fair play. Under Islam, the ends cannot justify the means. Individuals are reminded that they cannot make decisions for maximizing their personal welfare if such decisions are injurious to others.

Zaman outlines the various ways and means by which Islam promotes economic justice. He discusses the institutions of *al Zakah* (levy to purify wealth), *al Sadaqah* (charity), *al 'Irth* (the laws of inheritance), the *Bait al Mal* (the Public Treasury), and the role of the state. He then discusses whether or not Muslim states such as Malaysia, Pakistan, and Saudi Arabia (each with a distinctive type of political system, different resource endowments, and at a different stage of economic development), pursue policies to implement Islamic economic precepts and, thereby, promote economic justice. He concludes that a modest beginning has been made in these countries to implement some of the tenets of Islamic economic systems.

In chapter 5, "The Islamic Call: Social Justice and Political Realism," Tamara Sonn asserts that Islam, unlike Judaism and Christianity, calls for universal justice. She also asserts that the enforcement of Islamic ethics was possible in a world where Islam dominated the socioeconomic and cultural aspects of people's lives in non–nation states. She argues that today's nation states, dominated by the secular West, are anathema to the Islamic call for justice. According to her, Islamic jurists often in the past repudiated caliphs or rulers for straying "from the purity of the Islamic message." Yet it is the same jurisprudence which is now being used to disapprove overthrowing of stable regimes no matter how they deviate from religious teachings. The call of the activists to abandon secularism and to install governments that support *Shari'ah* rule do not jell well with the political realities of the Muslim world. Sonn is encouraged by "New Left" Muslim intellectuals who foresee the coexistence of secularism and religion. She insists that "it is the work of these realists which, therefore, provides the brightest hope for the fulfillment of the call for universal social justice."

In chapter 6, "Vicegerency and Gender Justice in Islam," Nimat Hafez Barazangi discusses the concept and the implications of human vicegerency to God on family life, especially relationships between males and females. She argues that the majority of Muslims "practice the principle of viceregency on an exposition level (such as political leadership), not at the essence level (in which each individual is taking the responsibility for executing the trust, the pontifex uniting Heavans and earth)." As such, Muslims can neither truly fulfill their responsibility, nor the central concept of Islam, *Tawhid,* that asserts the Oneness of God as the source of value and humanity as the moral being endowed with the ability to make a choice. Barazangi states that *Tawhid* implies that an Islamic value system that does not owe its source to the will of God, will cause injustice. Furthermore, an individual who cannot make a choice as to whether or not to execute the will of God is in essence not acting as a moral being who can understand the will enough to apply it as a system. Thus, inequality in the *Ummah*[2] (universal community), and within the family—particularly in gender relationships—stands in the way to fulfillment of God's will and this, in turn, prevents the realization of vicegerency on earth. She cites the position of some Islamic *Faqihs* (jurists) who ruled Friday's congregational prayer unobligatory for women as an example of one inequality, "a particularism on the meaning of vicegerency" which has prevented women not only from the mosques, but also from taking equal roles in the community and in executing the trust.

The critics of Islam go as far as to blame Islamic teachings for the persistent gender inequalities in Muslim societies, even though the source of such "teachings" lie in misinterpretations of the *Shari'ah*. Barazangi criticizes both the *Muqallidun* (imitators of precedent rulings by a specific school of *Fiqh* or jurisprudence) and modernists who took up the issue of women's attendance in mosques as a sign of either public *Fitna* (chaos) or achieving gender equality respectively. She is equally critical of both "liberated" and "*Muqallidun*" women who "take other's legislation as their source of value." Such women do not strive to learn the source materials on Islamic value nor choose to practice these values by themselves within the Islamic framework. Barazangi also emphasizes that the Quranic verse which refers to "the men and women both having a degree of advantage vis-à-vis each other" is often interpreted by many to mean "for men a degree over women" and out of its context to impose men's superiority over women. She urges the women to utilize their natural endowments to fulfill their religious and civil viceregency, since God has endowed all people with willpower and freedom of choice to be *Khalifat Allah* (God's vicegerent). Concurrently, she reminds men that women also have individual responsibility in Islam and that developing autonomous spiritual and intellectual Muslim identity among females is as essential as it is among males.

The first three chapters of part 2 concentrate on various aspects of Islamic justice in practice as propagated by Muslim scholars, jurists, and the Muslim states themselves. Chapter 7, "The Nuclear Option and International Justice: Islamic Perspectives" by Ali A. Mazrui, demonstrates how the Western powers, especially France, the United States, and Great Britain, conspired with Israel, and through it with South Africa, to deprive the Muslim world and Black Africa from acquiring nuclear capabilities, thereby weakening Africa's legitimate place in the community of nations. Mazrui details the conspiracy to nuclearize Israel and its partner South Africa to foster mutual goals of building nuclear arsenals to keep neighboring states under their domination. He argues that a horizontal nuclear proliferation (among countries such as Pakistan, Iraq, Libya, and Nigeria), along with a deceleration of vertical proliferation (in which the superpowers slowed their development and deployment of nuclear arsenals), will eventually lead to the end of the nuclear race. Mazrui suggests that the revolutionary zeal of Islam, combining the richness of some of the African member states with the scientific knowhow of the others, may make it possible for South Africa to achieve nuclear independence. The threat of nuclear proliferation by the Muslim world along with its African axis in Nigeria, Libya and black-ruled South Africa may be the catalyst needed to stop the nuclear race or, at least, make the world as a whole militarily safer.

Mazrui also discusses the revolutionary forces of Marxism in general and the Soviet Union in particular. Since both are essentially extinct now in Europe, the injustice of the power imbalance between the Muslim world and Africa on the one hand, and the Northern world and its client state Israel in the Middle East on the other, may begin to be alleviated.

A brief note on the transliteration and translation of Arabic/Islamic words and Quranic verses is in order here. To maintain a consistent transliteration, the editors primarily followed Isma'il Raji al Faruqi's system,[3] using diacritical marks only for ayn and hamza.

For the translation of Quranic quotations, the editors primarily used Abdullah Yousuf Ali's *Translation and Commentary*.[4] Exceptions include chapter 5, where the author, Tamara Sonn, followed A. J. Arberry's translation,[5] and chapter 1, in which author Fazlur Rahman provided his own translations. Because of Rahman's sudden death, the editors did not have the chance to consult with him about the context of his chapter. Thus, responsibility for any errors lies with the editors and not with the author.

It is important to remember that certain translations of Arabic words may have been influenced by the perspectives of the translators. For example, translating the word *Islam* as "submission" envisions God-human relations hierarchically, paralleling class, racial, and gender relationships.[6] Translations of *Islam* as "at peace" or "being on the right course" are derived from the root *Salama* (Quran 2:31, 3:20) but are rarely mentioned in contemporary literature.

Notes

1. Majid Khadduri, *The Islamic Conception of Justice* (Baltimore and London: Johns Hopkins University Press, 1984).

2. Isma'il Raji al Faruqi, "The Nation-State and Social Order in the Perspective of Islam," in *Trialogue of the Abrahamic Faiths*, edited by Isma'il Raji al Faruqi (Ann Arbor: New Era Publications, 1986), 47–59, distinguishes between *Ùmmah* (the universal community as the basis of human association) and *ùmmah* (the Muslim community). The Muslim community is only a segment of the universal community.

3. Isma'il Raji al Faruqi, *Toward Islamic English* (Ann Arbor: New Era Publications, 1986).

4. Abdullah Yousuf Ali, *The Holy Qur'an: Text, Translation, and Commentary* (N.p.: McGregor and Werner, 1946).

5. A. J. Arberry, *The Koran Interpreted* (New York: Macmillan, 1955).

6. Sachiko Murata, *The Tao of Islam: A Source Book on Gender Relationships in Islamic Thought* (Albany: State University of New York Press, 1992).

Part One

Justice:
The Ideals

Chapter One

Islam's Origin and Ideals

Fazlur Rahman

Socioeconomic Conditions and Religious Beliefs in Mecca and Arabia

The birth of Islam is well documented in recorded history. Its prophet, Muhammad (PBUH), son of Abdullah, was born in Makkah (Mecca) in 570. He died in 632. We have little knowledge of his life before his call to prophethood except that he was respected as a trusted person and often retired to a cave called Hira north of Mecca. In Hira, the Prophet contemplated the problems of life and death, particularly those that bedeviled Meccan society. Mecca, which was essentially commercial, had two major problems: polytheism (idol worship) and the city rulers—a rich, aristocratic tribe called Quraysh.

Mecca suffered from extreme socioeconomic inequality based on a thriving underground world of slaves and hirelings. This troubled the Prophet's mind, as the Quran shows. Addressing Muhammad (PBUH), the Quran says, "Alam nashrah laka sadrak" (Have we not now opened up your breast?) (94:1), an Arabic idiom for the solution, *Sharh al sadr* (a tormenting intellectual or spiritual problem). The Quran continues: "Alladhi anqada zahrak" (Have we not relieved that burden that was breaking your back?) (94:2).

The Quranic verses, particularly the early ones, condemn Meccan polytheism and city residents' general social irresponsibility. The Meccans, however, claimed they had earned their wealth and that neither the Prophet nor anyone else had the right to ask them to spend it in ways they disliked. "Why should we pay for the poor? God can feed them if He wants," they asserted.

According to the Quran, Christians and Jews had attempted to convert the Meccans before the advent of Islam. But these attempts had not been successful because the Meccans wanted "a new guidance whereby we will do better than these two communities—Jews and Christians. We don't want to convert to Judaism or Christianity." The Quran taunts their disbelief: "Now that dispensation has come, why don't you believe in it?" These attempts at conversion are one reason for Meccans' familiarity with Judeo-Christian ideas. When the Quran talks about the day of resurrection (the day of judgment), the Meccans reply, "We have heard of this before. The Jews and Christians told us there was going to be a day, but it's nothing but fables." The Quran clearly indicates the presence of these religious developments before Islam.

The Concept of God in Islam

The first revelation to Muhammad (PBUH) came during his contemplation at Hira. The essence of the message was "There is one God and one humanity." The Meccan mercantile aristocracy rejected the Prophet's teaching because they saw it as a double threat to their interests. First, it threatened their idol worship, particularly the idols stored in the *Ka'abah* (the cubed-shaped sanctuary in Mecca) that were the object of Arab pilgrimage. During this annual pilgrimage, Meccans earned a great deal of money from the pilgrims; and they feared losing this source of income if Muhammad (PBUH) succeeded in his preaching. Second, the aristocracy were threatened by the Prophet's insistence that the rich take care of the poor. The Quran contends that wealth does not belong entirely to the rich. *Haqqun Ma'lum* (a definite portion) belongs to those without wealth. But the Meccans asserted, "No, we have earned this. It is our right. Who are you to tell us how to spend it?" There were even more mundane reasons for Meccan opposition to the Prophet. For example, the Prophet belonged to the clan of Banu Hashim; and other clans feared that if they accepted him as the prophet of God, then Banu Hashim would rule the other clans forever.

Some of the poor and disenfranchised followed the Prophet, as did some well-to-do merchants—for example, Abu Bakr (d. 634). Yet his path was difficult. The Quran details his tribulations as he brought the message of Islam to the Meccans and the Medinites.

The word *Allah* (God) appears in the Quran some 2,500 times. As one tries to understand His meaning, it becomes clear that it is not important to know what God is but what He does and what His relationship to humanity is. The Quran is oriented to human beings and their private and public conduct. If there were one person in the world, I don't know what the Quran would tell him or her to do or think or how to behave. But the Quran is certain that when there is more than one human being, then God is there. A well-known verse in *Surat al Mujadalah* (a Quranic chapter, "The Argumentation") says, "Whenever there are three of you in trusted consultation, God is the fourth. Whenever there are five of you, God is the sixth. And whenever there is a lesser number or greater, God is there" (58:7). God is a dimension in human presence. He intervenes between person and person, and this is why the concept of human conduct vis-à-vis other humans is central in Quranic teaching.

The Concept of Taqwa in the Quran

There are three central terms in the Quran: *Iman* (faith); *Islam* (surrender to God, His will, or His law); and *Taqwa* (piety). If one analyzes these three terms, their meanings turn out to be identical. Iman is from the root *Amana* (to have peace, security, and amnesty from danger). Islam comes from the root *Salama* (to be whole; to be integral; to be at peace; not to disintegrate). Taqwa comes from the root *Waqi* (to save or protect from loss). A utensil that holds something is called *Waqiya* because it protects something from getting lost or wasted.

What do we have here? We have what I call the unconscious of the Quran. Because the meanings of these three terms are identical, I conclude that the basic thrust of the Quran is to enable humans to keep their individual and collective personalities intact—to save them from disintegration so that each person can move forward rather than disintegrate or get lost. This, I believe, is the function of God in the Quran. A verse in *Surat al Hashr* says: "wa la takunu ka alladhin nasw Allah" (don't be like those who forgot God) "fa ansahum anfusahum" (and [eventually] God made them forget their own souls) (59:19). Those who forgot were disintegrated; they were finished; they could not keep their self-worth. God is the dimension in human behavior that keeps humankind together. It is not a small matter that all three terms should share this meaning.

The first thing the Quran wants from humans is the inner state called Taqwa, often translated as piety. Taqwa appears in human action, including fear of God. There is no doubt that the Quran talks about this fear: "Those people who pray at night—when God is mentioned, their hearts palpitate" (8:1–2). Yet fear is not the only element in Taqwa. Rather, it embodies a consciousness of God that enables a person to behave responsibly. Muhammad Asad translates the word as "God consciousness," which is more correct than the common translation "piety." Yet piety is not wrong if one keeps the more complex meaning in mind. Taqwa involves a sense of responsibility.

The word has been used in both the Meccan and Medinese periods of the Quran but more commonly in the Medinese. More often than not, it appears during considerations of human behavior vis-à-vis other people. Thus, it becomes the main theme of the Quran at the political, social, family, and religious levels. At all these levels the Quran wants human beings to become responsible.

It is well known that Islam brings in no intermediaries between humans and God, so there is no intermediary to whom a Muslim entrusts his or her soul. Each person is answerable to God on the day of judgment. This day of judgment, this sense of responsibility, is what makes every person human. Of course, humans have the power of choice. The Quran tells this story: when God wanted to create Adam, the angels said, "Why are you creating this fellow? He is going to do evil, going to shed blood, and this and that. We are sufficient to glorify your presence." God, in answer, did not deny the charges of the angels against Adam but simply said, "I know what you don't know" (2:30). Then he brought the angels and Adam together and asked them about the names of things. The angels were not able to name things, but Adam was. Thus, humans have a creative power for knowledge.

But while our cognitive powers are great, the moral sense that should arise from these powers has not developed enough. It has not kept pace with our cognitive powers. Time and again, the Quran complains that humans have not kept up their original primordial covenant with God: an agreement to be good. This is the reason for the day of judgment. The day of judgment does not exist for donkeys or horses; it exists for humans because only human action is meaningful—only human action transcends itself. It carries its life beyond its performance. This is why the Quran talks so often about weighing deeds.

On the day of judgment, God will weigh deeds that today appear big but in the long run are absolutely meaningless. Deeds that may seem insignificant now, however, may be very weighty in the long run. The

Quran stresses the day of judgment as "al Ghayb, ʿAqibatu al Úmur" (the unknown; the end of affairs). It says, in essence:

> Keep your eye on the end of affairs. Don't act out of motivation for the here and now because that's what the animals do. Surely humans ought to know better. Your actions have weight or ought to have weight. If a human lives from day to day or hour to hour, he or she is no better than a donkey. That's why there is day of judgment. People say the day of judgment is a kind of addendum. It is not. It is central to the whole system of faith. In whatever form that judgment is to be carried out, it must be carried out. There is no doubt of it, and human nature cries for it.

A sense of responsibility, Taqwa, develops inside humans. It is a kind of a spiritual torch that shows us what we are doing and what we ought to do. Of course, if one develops Taqwa to the highest level, there is no need for judgment. Then every minute is judgment.

The Quran says that on the day of judgment we shall resurrect our inner self and confront every human with it. Then we shall see "Kunta fi ghaflatin min hadha" (You were heedless of all of this) "fa kashfna ʿanka gitaáka" (but we have now thrown away all the veils) "fa basaruka al yauma hadid" (so today your sight is very keen; you can see yourself) (50:22). Of course, the questions implied is "Why couldn't you see yourself when you were there?"

The Concept and Ideals of Justice in Islam

The words ʿAdl and *Qist* (justice; equity; fair play) abound in the Quran. They apply to both friends and enemies. Muslims were persecuted for years by their opponents in Mecca; and some, after the fall of Mecca, wanted to take revenge against their enemies. But two verses at the beginning of *Surat al Maida* say, "Let not the enmity of a people determine you upon a course of being wrongful to them. Don't be wrongful to them; be fair to them, because being fair is nearest to Taqwa" ("Aqrab ila al Taqwa") (5:9).

It is not possible here for me to sift through all the teachings that exist on social and economic justice. But we know that the Quran instituted *al Zakah* (a levy to purify wealth) for the welfare of the poor. The Prophet, when he came to Medina, instituted a system of brotherhood whereby the local population shared all they had with the immigrants: homes, wealth, hearts, fears, and so on. Islam has a tremendous emphasis on social and economic justice; and several other Islamic institutions that had no precedent have undertaken this mission. The *Awqaf,* an institution that endows schools, hospitals, wayfarers, and the poor, is one of these institutions. A lasting example of *Awqaf* is a huge hospital, built in the twelfth century in Cairo by the Mamluk ruler Mansur Qalawun, that is still treating the blind today. Its *Waqf* (sing. of *Awqaf,* religious endowment) document says,

> In this hospital patients shall be treated—locals and foreigners; men and women irrespective of race, religion, and color; old and young. Everyone will be treated, and particular attention shall be paid to the mentally sick because when a person loses his or her mind, they lose all their honor and Islam is basically concerned with protecting human honor and dignity.

This inspiration has remained with the Muslims, even when they have lost touch with the Quran.

The Quran says that God's guidance is not a prerogative of Jews, Christians, and Muslims. God has been sending his guidance to all humankind, to all peoples: "Wa li kulli qawmin had" (Every people has had its guide) (13:7). "Wa ín min úmmatin ílla khala fiha nadhir" (There is no people without a warner [from God] who has lived among them) (35:24). Of course, the Quran does not claim that all religions are the same. But the Quran asks, "Fa kaiyfa idha jína min kuli úmatin bishahid" (How then if we brought from each nation a witness [on judgment day]?) (4:41). In essence, then, if not in fact, religion is the same for all humanity. This is why the Quran says that the office of divine guidance is indivisible. You cannot create distinctions and separations between one prophet and the other. You cannot say, I'll believe in this prophet and not in others. Prophethood has to be believed in as a whole: "Amantu bi ma anzal Allahu min kitab" (I believe in any book God may have revealed, [whether I know it or not]) (42:15). Although guidance is universal, however, it may be distorted. The Quran accuses both Jews and Christians of doing wrong to their own teachings and claiming monopoly for divine guidance.

The Quran does not legislate for every human behavior whether it relates to 'Adl or to any other Islamic principle. Rather, it partly legislates and partly show the way for further development. When Islam spread to various lands, it was culturally influenced by those people. This cultural diversity, which grew further after the Prophet's death, formed the basic temperament of the Muslim community because of this Quranic flexibility. The Muslims were able to work out legal and social institutions and ran a great empire. Within Islam there was also an international, multifaith, multiethnic society, a forerunner of the modern world order. Islam, characterized in the Quran as *al Din* (a worldview and a way of life), was the first religious worldview in which Jew, Muslim, Christian, Zoroastrian, and Hindu could learn medicine, science, and poetry together.

Yet, because Islam was open to integrating many cultures, the Quranic dream of uniting humankind on a viable spiritual and egalitarian basis did not last long. Although the Quran invited Jews and Christians to share in this dream: "ya áhla al kitab" (oh, people of the Book) "ta'alau íla Kalimatin" (let us come to a formula) "sawaán baynana wa baynakum" (that will be common between you and us) (3:64), some of its teachings were distorted by both Muslims and non-Muslims. What the Prophet left to Muslims was to some extent elaborated, to some extent gravely distorted. The *Sunnah* (the path and example) of the Prophet is replete with elements that have nothing to do with him. They became part of Islam through its spread to other cultures.

A good example of these distortions is the distortion of the central teachings concerning equality between males and females. Equality of the sexes is instituted in the Quran (4:1, 7; 60:12; 49:10; 96:1–4) for a Muslim society to achieve 'Adl and Quist. In Islam, equality between males and females as partners in family life characterizes social life at large. The Quran explains the position of women in detail. It is not true that the woman in *Jahiliyah* (the days of ignorance; a reference to pre-Islamic practices) had a very low position, although many Muslim preachers have tried to give their audiences this impression. Certainly there is no doubt that women were subject to certain abuses. For example, infant girls were buried alive for both economic reasons and reasons of honor. But there were also women like Khadijah (the Prophet's wife), who owned a business. The Quran streamlined the sex life of Arabia in women's favor when it instituted marriage. Its prohibition of *Akhdan* (partners in free love) was not intended to restrict women's sex life. Rather, the *Khidn* practice (sing. of *Akhdan*, a man or a woman who has a sexual partner without being married) left many women without rights to inheritance, to child custody, and so on, and Islam instituted these rights as part of its reform for social justice. Being culturally influenced by other peoples' views of women, some of these Quranic and Prophetic teachings were confused with societal customs of these peoples and were malpracticed, sometimes in the name of Islam.

Chapter Two

The Islamic Concept of Justice

Mahmoud Ayoub

Quranic Terms for Justice

In this chapter I discuss several aspects of justice in Islam: justice in faith, theology, law, and politics; and justice as a moral principle. In the Quran and, hence, in later tradition, two basic words, *'Adl* and *Qist,* broadly translate as "justice." 'Adl in Islam means a balanced approach to all things, including life. Therefore, 'Adl or 'Adil also is a reference to a person who is morally, behaviorally, and spiritually balanced. Qist, on the other hand, refers to the way in which Muslims deal with one another and God deals with us. According to the Quran, God establishes Qist, or justice: "Shahida Allahu ánnahu la ilah illa Hawa wa al malaíkatu wa úlu al 'ilm" (God bears witness that there is no God but He, and so do the angels and those endowed with knowledge), "Qaíman bil Qist" ([God] is standing firm on justice) (3:18). Qist essentially concerns human social interaction, if we use the term to include both God and humans in this interchange. It includes the notion of fairness in dealing with others.

The Concept of *al Wasat* or a Middle Course

Two subsidiary Islamic terms define the concept of justice: *al Nasf* and *al Wasat*. Al Nasf (or *al Nasafa*) implies sharing in equity. It means dividing something into two equal portions. Hence, justice in Islam is a way of relating to one another without having anyone come up short. The second term, *Wasat,* appears in the Quran in this sense: "Wa kadhalika ja'alnakum úmmatan wasata letakunu shuhadaá 'ala al nas" (Thus have we made you a community of the *Wasat*, meaning middle course, that you may be witnesses over human kind) (2:143).

Islam is basically a religion of education—a pedagogical system. I, for one, do not apologize for anything that has developed within Muslim history. The Muslim world is all good, and the problems that have arisen do not mean we have or have not followed a single source or a majority of sources. The problems are very complex, and following the Quran means many things to many people at different times. Without our wealth of culture, philosophy, science, and theology, Islam would have been a simple religion, little developed beyond the *Hunafá*, the righteous people of Arabia before Islam. We would not have had a civilization. For everything we pay a price.

Wasat means that whatever we develop ought to be developed with a sense of fair, middle ground. Most Quranic commentators take verse 2:143 to mean "in the middle between the too-much and the too-little": that is, between *Ifrat* and *Tafrit*. Most commentators also relate Wasat to faith. In other words, to be a person or a community of the middle course means that we do not relegate God to a distant status, as the Arabs before Islam did. Those Arabs were not exactly polytheists in the sense that they took other gods as equal to God.[1] They might not have considered them equal, but (to use the Quranic phrase) they did not give God the measure of respect that is due to Him: "Maqaddaru Allaha haqqa quadrih" (6:91, 22:74, 39:67). In that sense, then, they were on the minus side of the middle course. In contrast, the commentators say that Christians were on the too-much side of the middle course because they associated others with God, such as Jesus Christ, his mother, and the holy spirit. Therefore, just faith, in accordance with al Wasat, means to have a faith that is reflected in a balanced life. Some commentators believe the word Wasat also means 'Adl: that is, a middle course in one's behavior—not to pray too much or not at all but only as much as required and one is capable of. The Aristotelian mean is very close to Wasat, except that Wasat adds the element of faith.

'Adl According to the *Mu'tazilite* and *Shi'ite* Philosophies

'Adl means "to be upright" or, as the Quran says, "to be straight in one's dealings." Some Muslim groups made the concept so important that it became a primary principle of faith. Two such groups, the *Mu'tazilite* and the *Shi'ite*, have left an important legacy in their understanding of justice, which bears very much on modern Muslim viewpoints. (I am referring here to the moderate *Shi'ite*, the twelve *Imami Shi'ite*, a group that developed a definite theology and system of jurisprudence.

According to the *Mu'tazilite*, justice was one of the basic attributes of God. It became one of the important five principles that distinguish the group's emphasis from that of other Muslims. For them, and later for the *Shi'ite*, God's justice meant that He could not do anything that was not best for His creatures. In a sense, then, God was constrained by His own attribute of justice.

If God can do nothing *Qabih* (bad) but only *Hasan* (good), how are we to account for the evil in the world? According to both the *Shi'ite* and the *Mu'tazilite*, human beings are the authors of their own actions; therefore, they are responsible for the good or bad of their actions. God only provides the basis for good things. This concept relates in *Shi'ite* Islam to the notion of leadership and authority. It is God's justice that He does not leave His creatures without guidance, not only during the period of revelation (that is, from Adam to Muhammad [PBUH]) but also after, when qualified individuals or groups will need to interpret and implement the divine word of the Quran and prophetic tradition. This act (of God's not leaving His creatures without guidance) is regarded as an expression of divine *Lutf* (grace), which is also an expression of divine *Rahma* (mercy), which also is an expression of divine 'Adl (justice). An understanding of this principle is vital to an understanding of what has happened in Iran.

Qist and the Idea of Social Justice

Qist relates theologically to God's purposes in creation. The most important verse concerning this concept is found in Surah 3 of the Quran. Verse 18 (which I quoted earlier) reads: "God bears witness that there is no God but He, and so do the angels and those endowed with knowledge: [God] is standing firm on justice." Here God's Qist means that He created a fair world—a world that has no flaw, as the Quran says—and has laid down certain obligations for people to follow to maximize the harmony between creation and humanity. Hence, those who best understand and appreciate God's justice are those endowed with knowledge. Qist is also related to the notion of fairness, of goodness. That is, God does not oppress.

We can perhaps understand Qist better by relating the word to its opposite. In Islam *Zulm* is the opposite of 'Adl or Qist. Interestingly, Zulm is related etymologically to the notion of darkness, opaqueness, and gloom. It means "to deny or deprive oneself of a basic right." One can be just, or 'Adil, or establish Qist with oneself or with someone else. Conversely, one can do wrong to oneself or be *'Idl* (unjust) with others. Zulm is often interpreted as oppression, but it means far more. It goes back to the Islamic notion of justice that implies sharing. Zulm is to get a bigger share than your fellow human being, which creates opacity, darkness, and confusion.

More than 'Adl, Qist relates specifically to social relations among human beings. For example, one can show Qist, or justice, in the way one buys and sells. Therefore, the Quran says, "Wa áqimu al wazn bil qist" (So establish justice with balance, with fairness) "wa la tukhsiru al mizan" (and do not err in the balance [cheat in weights]) (55:9). Qist means acting fairly with others. As the Quran says, "God does not forbid you, regarding those who do not fight with you on account of your faith nor drive you out of your home, from dealing kindly and justly [with Qist] toward them, for God loves those who establish Qist (Inna Allaha yuhebbu al muqsitin)" (60:8). Qist, then, is social justice in its broadest sense—first in our relationship to God and second in our relationship to society. The concept has both theological and religious implications.

'Adl and the Idea of a Just Law

With regard to law, however, 'Adl is more relevant than Qist. It is often related to two areas: the judgment of a *Qadi* (judge) and the testimony of a *Shahid* (witness). A Qadi who is an 'Adil is one who is always afraid of committing wrong against others. Examples of such Qadis are frequent in Muslim history. Abu Hanifa (d. 767), one of the great jurists of the Muslim community, refused to accept the office of a judge even though he was imprisoned and beaten every day until he died. He refused the office, not because he lacked the capacity to judge, but because he was afraid that he might not be a good judge. He also believed that the political apparatus was corrupt; therefore, even if he tried to establish 'Adl, he might not be able to do so. Ja'far al Sadiq, a contemporary of Abu Hanifa, once said: "Scholars are the trustees of the messengers, until they turn to the sultan [come under the influence of the ruler]. Once they do so, then suspect them."[2]

Thus, justice can be understood as an ideal situation in which balance in judgment is so important yet so difficult to achieve that one may choose to do nothing—at least in Abu Hanifa's case. Yet not everyone in the Muslim community followed his lead. We know Abu Hanifa so well only because his students, who did take high state offices, wrote down and elaborated on his otherwise unrecorded legal statements and queries.

With regard to the witness, the Quran uses the concept of justice in a public sense. It alludes to two major concerns: marriage problems and financial transactions. For example, to arbitrate between an estranged husband and wife, people should "take for witness two persons from among you, endowed with justice and establish the evidence [as] before God" (65:2). When speaking of financial transactions, the Quran states: "O ye who believe when you deal with each other, in transactions involving future obligations in a fixed period of time, reduce them to writing, let a just scribe write down faithfully as between the parties" (2:282). Here, also, people who are just are called upon to witness.

In other difficult situations where people are in conflict, witnesses are called on who are declared to be pure. This notion of *Tazkiya* (purifying) is the source of the word *Zakat*. In such situations, people in the society agree and declare to a judge that X and Y are pure, trustworthy people; therefore, their testimony can be accepted. These witnesses have been praised as persons of 'Adl.

Although I have simplified my explanation of Tazkiya (which can be a complex legal issue), I am trying to explain that however we look at the terms *just* or *justice* in Islam, we come back to the notion that they are equivalent to piety or uprightness. Thus, a variety of terms that must be included in the description of a person's justice: *Taqwa* (piety), *Istiqama* (uprightness), *Ihsan* (goodness), *Salah* (righteousness) *Salih* (a person who does good) and so on. As Quran shows, they are not elaborated laws but moral imperatives and broad guidelines that allow a tradition to develop.

Sociopolitical Justice in Islam

Justice in Islam is both individual and public. Individual justice is open only to God to know. In this case, the opposite of 'Adl is *Israf* (extravagance): "O my servants who have been too extravagant toward yourselves, your souls, do not despair of God's mercy; for God forgives all sins" (39:53). This idea may have been the basis of the Hadith (the authentic traditions of Prophet Muhammad [PBUH]) in which the Prophet asserts that when a person says "La Ilaha Illa Allah" (There is no god but God Almighty), he or she means far more than a simple statement.[3] In the same way, God's mercy is far bigger than all our sins, however great they may be. So Abu Dharr, I hope, was pleasantly surprised when the Prophet told him that he would go to Paradise even if he committed sins. We do not organize an inquisition to judge a person's morality. Rather, we have a pedagogical system to establish and uplift the moral life of the community.

Justice is required in even greater measure when it relates to one of the most grievous public offenses in Islam: adultery. Here, not two but four witnesses are required. If they cannot establish the veracity of their testimony, then they are punished.

'Adl in politics is a complex issue, one that I must preface with a controversial statement: while the Quran provides clear if broad moral guidelines for the life of the individual and the community, neither the Quran nor the Prophet left us a clear political model to follow. I believe that the political model adopted by the Muslims after the Prophet's death was devised quickly. It was so good that it worked for many centuries and remains the ideal system to this day. But the system is broad, and it works best when the people who head it have moral integrity—are morally just people.

For instance, the first caliph, Abu Bakr, took three dirhams from the central treasury of the Muslims every day. He spent this tiny sum on himself and his family because he could no longer attend to his own gardens or earn his own living. Thus, he took what amounted to a small wage. The third caliph, 'Uthman (d. 656), argued that if everybody received his or her share, what was it to anyone if the caliph did whatever he wished with the rest? And with the rest he sometimes did a great deal. For example, he married his daughter to a man to whom he gave one hundred thousand dirhams. When the treasurer of the Central Islamic Treasury objected, 'Uthman said, "You are only our treasurer." But the treasurer replied, "No, if I am your treasurer, then I resign. I am the treasurer of the Muslims." 'Uthman was a good leader compared to some who came after him.

The Prophet could serve as a political model only in a limited way. What he did was guided directly by God. We see the Quran often objecting to and correcting his actions. Thus, Islamic order during the Prophet's time was actually a theocracy. After him, it was a nomocracy:

that is, an order based on law. Just laws had to be devised, but they were devised not on the basis of what *ought* to be but on what had to happen post facto in the Muslim community.

For example, the Quran calls for *Shura* (mutual consultation) among the Muslims. Later, Islamic political theorists such as Al Mawardi (974?–1058) had to justify actions that led to the election of the first caliph—a limited Shura of those "who had the authority to bind and loosen" (Ahl al Hall wa-al 'Aqd). Theorists also had to justify the appointment of one caliph by another, as Abu Bakr appointed 'Umar (d. 644): not on the basis of clear Islamic principle but on the basis of precedence.

In times of difficulty in the Middle Ages and perhaps in contemporary situations, the justification of whatever oppression and corruption exists today, what was required of the ruler was not justice but rather strength. Once a ruler achieves power, it becomes the basis for the legitimacy of his rule. His rule becomes legitimate not because he acts justly (although if he does, that is good) but because he is able to defend the integrity of the Muslim community. Hence, as Al Ghazzali said, a hundred years of injustice (Zulm) are better than a day of chaos. Such an attitude led the Muslim community to idealize the principle of political justice as a messianic goal that depends on the coming of a *Mahdi*. A Mahdi is a ruler guided by God who will come to earth and replace injustice and inequity with 'Adl. This belief is so general in Islam that some Muslim thinkers have said that anyone who rejects the Hadith relating to the Mahdi must be regarded as a *Kafir* (rejecter of faith).[4] (Some have wanted to reject the Hadith of the Mahdi because it was transmitted as "Akhbar al Áhad" [on a single authority].)

Many rulers in Muslim history have claimed the title and prerogative of a Mahdi and have promised such an ideal state. But the notion may reach its highest expression in the Shi'ite idea of the hidden *Imam*—a religious leader who epitomizes that which is good and just throughout human history. In other words, he is the other side of all that has gone wrong. Because he is in the world, it benefits from his presence. But divine power conceals him from view until God in His good pleasure wills the Imam to appear and right all wrongs in faith, theology, and politics.

Of course, the ideal of the Mahdi is a psychological answer to a long history of frustration in the Shi'ite community. (The only acceptable ruler of the *Shi'ite* community was 'Ali (d. 661), the fourth caliph, who ruled for four years.) The ideal of the Imam can only be realized when the world is about to end. The Mahdi will rule for seven years or seventy years; and forty days after his death, the resurrection will come. In the past this notion led to quietism, but more recently it has been reinterpreted within Iran's violent Islamic revolution. In the long run, this revolution will be remembered as one of the most interesting and important events in the twentieth century because its success will create many repercussions. If it fails, however, the whole ideal of Shi'ite Mahdism will also be smashed.

The ideal of future utopian justice has helped preserve the community and given it a kind of moral support and basis. Thus, after every prayer the Shi'ites say, "O God we beseech you for a noble state or society in which you will give honor and glory to Islam and its people, and dishonor and humility to the people of hypocrisy and to hypocrisy itself." Here, ideal justice is expressed as a mythical future, not a mythical past. This contrasts with the Sunni concept of ideal justice, which is based on a mythical past. But if we examine this past, we find it far less ideal than myth would claim, principally because we did not have a clear political model to follow. Muslims have said, and with good reason, that Islam is a complete religion: it includes politics, economics, faith, and much more. In reality, however, there are limits to this assertion. We, Muslims, all grope for an ideal that perhaps we were expected to establish, but were unable to.

As I see it, then, the principle of justice means many things to many people—whether or not they follow the Quran. The problems of justice that arise are problems of society in the Muslim world, which has no cohesive leadership. We have no one to speak for all of us, perhaps because, both literally and figuratively, we all speak different languages.

Notes

1. *Editors' note:* Dr. Ayoub seems to emphasize here that the Arabs believed in one ruling God and several minor ones. This may seem contradictory to the way Muslims in general understand the condition of Arabia before the birth of Islam. The author's explanation that the Arabs did not give God His due respect, however, indicates a fine theological differentiation from Fazlur Rahman's statement in chapter 1, not a different conception of God.

2. Abdul al Rasul al Wa'idhi, 'Ashi'ah: Min Balaghat al Imam al sadiq (Beirut: Mu'assasat al Nur lil Matbu'at, 1988), 149.

3. Muhammad bin 'Abdu Allah al Khatib al 'Umari al Tabrizi, *Mishkat al Masabih*, vol. 1, ed. M. Nasir al Din al Albani (Damascus: al Maktab al Islami, 1961); Kitab al Iman, p. 15; Hadith: 26.

4. Tabrizi, *Mishkat al Masabih*, vol. 3; Kitab al Fitan, p. 24, Hadith 5454.

Chapter Three

Comparative View of Justice

I. The Concept of Justice in Judaism
Laurence Edwards

Torah and the Rabbinic Interpretation of Justice
For many centuries, in many places, Jews have lived as a minority without full political power to apply and develop Jewish law. Yet the legal sections of Torah were clearly intended as a workable code for a specific society and indeed served as such through most of the biblical period.[1] Torah's later interpreters, the rabbis, based their claim to authority on an unbroken chain of tradition reaching all the way back to Moses. Torah itself clearly indicates that there is an oral tradition of interpretation (which, according to the rabbis, was given to Moses at the same time as the written Torah).

Even without independence, most Jewish communities did have a certain amount of internal autonomy. If Jewish concepts of justice could not be fully realized in life, they nevertheless formed the subject of extensive (and intensive) study—itself a religious act. In that context, rabbinic discussion, interpretation, and application of Jewish law has been a complex balancing act: What is the ideal? What is realistically feasible? What are people able to do?

The notion that God is just, as contrasted with the apparent capriciousness of pagan gods, was an appealing feature of monotheism. *Midat Hadin* (God's justice) is balanced by *Midat Harahamim* (God's mercy), although there is no exact formula for balancing the two. A *Midrash* (rabbinic interpretation) of the biblical story of creation suggests that God at first wanted to create the world through the attribute of strict justice but realized that the world could not exist on those terms. Therefore, he combined it with mercy.

Terms of Justice in Judaism

The various Hebrew words that denote justice are sometimes used interchangeably. More often, however, they have distinct connotations. *Tsedeq* (righteousness) usually refers to the abstract ideal of justice. An example is the often misunderstood *Lex Talionis* (eye for eye, tooth for tooth [Exodus 21:24–25]), a pure justice generally unrealized in practice and probably never intended to be taken literally. Examples of more applicable principles appear, among other places, in Leviticus 19:

> You shall not coerce your neighbor. You shall not commit robbery. The wages of a laborer shall not remain with you until morning. You shall not insult the deaf, or place a stumbling block before the blind. You shall fear your God: I am the Lord. You shall not render an unfair decision: do not favor the poor or show deference to the rich; judge your neighbor fairly. . . . When a stranger resides with you in your land, you shall not wrong him. The stranger who resides with you shall be to you as one of your citizens; you shall love him as yourself, for you were strangers in the land of Egypt: I the Lord am your God. (vv. 13–15, 33–34)

The term *Mishpat,* sometimes translated as "judgment," often connotes the procedural aspects of justice, which are obviously crucial in attempting to realize the ideal. The Talmud is replete with detailed descriptions of court procedures, including rules of evidence, witnesses, the prohibition of self-incrimination, even the seating arrangements for the judges. The rabbis also stress the importance of the appearance of justice as well as justice itself. For example, a judge who might remotely seem to have some personal interest in a case must remove himself from the trial proceedings.

From the Judaic point of view, the establishment and proper functioning of law courts are so important to human society that they are considered part of the seven *Noachide* laws—laws derived from the covenant that God made with Noah after the flood and thus applicable to not only Jews but all humankind. Torah discusses in several places the creation of legal institutions (especially Exodus 18 and Deuteronomy 16) and makes clear the connection between procedural and ideal justice. "You shall appoint magistrates and clerks for your tribes, in all the settlements that the Lord is giving you, and they shall govern the people with righteous judgment (Mishpat Tsedeq). You shall not judge unfairly: you shall show no partiality; you shall not take bribes, for bribes blind the eyes of the discerning and upset the plea of the just. Justice, justice (Tsedeq Tsedeq) shall you pursue, that you may thrive and occupy the land that the Lord your God is giving you." (Deuteronomy 15:18–20) This connection between Tsedeq and Mishpat is also nicely reflected in a verse from Psalms (94:15), in which the hope is expressed that "judgment (Mishpat) will again conform with justice (Tsedeq)."

The verse continues, "and all the upright in heart (*Yoshrei lev*) shall follow it." The word here translated as "upright" derives from the Hebrew *Yosher*, literally "straightness," itself a synonym for justice. The word is most often applied to an individual who seeks to live justly. Such a person will often act *lifnim mishurat hadin,* going beyond the strict letter of the law in order to be scrupulously fair.

This is a very brief sketch of justice as it is understood in Judaism—conceptually, institutionally, and individually. The principles of justice derived from Torah have been worked out in great detail but have never been fully put into practice. They have, however, informed much of Jewish life over the centuries and have influenced non-Jewish societies as well. In recent years, although the texts remain the same, contexts have been radically altered. The impact of modernity on Jewish life and Jewish concepts of justice is a vast subject in itself, one that we can do no more than mention here.

The last two centuries have witnessed major dislocations, and even destruction, of many traditional Jewish communities. With the loosening of external constraints on Jewish life, especially in the West, and the consequent exposure to new ideas and new opportunities, has come the breakdown of the authority of rabbinic courts and other traditional institutions. Recent developments also include the rise of nationalism and its Jewish version, Zionism. The largest Jewish community in the world today is in North America and is participating in the great American experiment in pluralistic democracy. What is astonishing is how relevant many of the ancient concepts of justice continue to be. Even when they are not directly applicable, the underlying principles seem as sound as ever.

II. A Christian Understanding of Justice: Reflections for an Interfaith Discussion

Byron Lee Haines

The character of justice in a pluralistic society is a subject that needs to be explored if Muslims, Jews, and Christians are to cooperate well and peaceably in American society. In considering the Christian understanding of justice, one must recognize that Christians have different opinions among themselves about what justice entails. This discussion, therefore, represents only one point of view. In spite of differences, however, there are major areas of agreement.

In the United States, justice tends to be associated with the law of the land. Christians in America support that association, and only in extreme circumstances do they advocate violation of that law. In the New Testament, the apostle Paul says, "Let every person be subject to the governing authorities" and explains that resisting such authorities is resisting God (13:1–3). The law as determined by the governing authorities must therefore be obeyed so that society maintains order and establishes justice for all its people insofar as it can.

On the other hand, Christians in certain circumstances have claimed that certain laws support social structures and practices that they consider contrary to the justice that God demands. Some have openly broken those laws in the name of Christian justice. These Christians have cited Paul in defense of their disobedience. In Galatians, for example, Paul speaks of Christians who are freed from slavery to law by virtue of the new understanding of righteousness that God has revealed through Christ. The reason for this disobedience lies in the Christian recognition that justice and its realization in the human situation involve matters so complex that they cannot be covered by either the law of the land (or any legal system, for that matter) or governing authorities.

The Substance of Justice

The explanation for Christian disobedience lies in certain beliefs that Christians have about justice. These beliefs have their origin in the nature of the Christian commitment to God through Christ, in the Scripture, and in the traditions of the Church. But before I discuss these ruling concepts, I must mention a matter of terminology. Within the biblical tradition, the idea of justice is covered by the term *righteousness*. Justice is, therefore, that which results when people do what is right. Within this context, justice and righteousness are interchangeable.

There are three basic Christian beliefs about the nature of righteousness. First, the origin of righteousness lies in the character and nature of God. Because God is righteous (that is, God does what is right), human beings, as creatures of God, are to be righteous. Whatever Christians understand about righteousness is intimately related to their understanding of the character of God.

This basic understanding about the origin of righteousness has several implications. For one thing, it means that, in the search for righteousness in human social structures, ultimate human allegiance is not to human authority but God's authority—the authority against which all other authorities are pale, derivative shadows. The justice enjoyed by a human society should not be something that human beings work out by and for themselves on the basis of what they suppose to be humanistic values. Rather, justice is what human beings work out in light of what they understand to be demanded of them by the righteousness of God. Thus, Martin Luther could oppose certain practices and claims of the Church by appealing to the authority of the righteousness of God. Many Christians have fought against civil governments when they felt that those governments stood in opposition to the righteousness that God requires. Certainly, this was the case during the Civil War, when some American Christians opposed slavery, and during World War II, when some German Christians opposed Nazism and its atrocities.

Because righteousness has its origin in the nature of God, Christians also believe that all righteousness or justice is a gift characterized by the grace and mercy of God. Human effort in the realization of a just society is fragmentary at best. Ultimately, the achievement of a righteous society is dependent upon God's grace—manifested in what God has done for us in the past, is doing for us now, and will do for us in the future. When Christians talk about justice, they are talking about not only what they struggle to realize in the present but also hope for in the future, when all human effort will be realized in the grace and mercy of God.

The second basic belief about righteousness is derived from the first. The norms for determining what is right (or the substance of righteousness) originate in divine revelation. To look elsewhere would be a denial of God's grace. For Christians, the divine revelation is revealed in God's word to all human beings. To know how to live rightly, Christians look to the word of their Scriptures, the Old and New Testaments, and behind that word to the living word of God manifested in the person they call Jesus Christ. Because of this revelation, human beings are not left to grope blindly in the dark in a desperate effort to find the path upon which God would have them walk. God has given Christians what is essential to their efforts to achieve justice on earth.

In turning to the Scriptures for God's guidance, Christians find themselves described, in part, as a covenant community, living within a tradition that began with God's covenant with Abraham and found its final fulfillment in Christ. Within this tradition, Christians accept as definitive the covenant stipulations of Exodus and the prophets' applications of those stipulations to the life of the Israelite people. The Decalogue, or Ten Commandments (Exodus 20), is the primary and authoritative statement of these stipulations. Of those commandments, three have to do with the relationship between human beings and God; the remaining seven define relationships between human beings. These laws identify the kind of righteousness that God require of those who claim to live by his rule. Micah 6:8 summarizes the legal, ethical, and spiritual requirements of the Israelite covenant faith: "He has showed you, O people, what is good and what does the Lord require of you but to do righteousness, to love mercy, and to walk humbly with your God." One can point also to the many prophetic injunctions to feed the poor and the widowed, to avoid idolatry, to rule and judge fairly without bias and prejudice, to refrain from immorality and oppressive social practices such as lying, stealing and bribery that exploit and denigrate others, and to avoid religious ceremony if it is used as a substitute for right conduct.

It is possible to interpret the prophets' words as saying that the only justice available to the majority community is what it is willing to guarantee for the minority communities and for those without power in the society—the oppressed, the outcasts, the weak, the fewest in number. Furthermore, if the laws of society do not guarantee all citizens the equality, integrity, and dignity of life that are required in God's sight, then that law is unrighteous. All these insights into the nature of righteous living come from the word of God revealed in the early covenant traditions, and they give normative shape and content to the Christian understanding of righteousness.

For Christians, the covenant tradition finds its fullest exposition and meaning in the life and ministry of Jesus Christ. Christians believe that, because of what God accomplished in Jesus Christ, the earlier covenant traditions are validated. Moreover, Jesus himself, by virtue of his complete obedience to God, embodies all that the covenant obligations intended to accomplish. Thus, the hope for righteousness contained in the covenant is clearly revealed in a new way and authenticated for Christians in the person of Jesus Christ.

How this is all worked out within the life of the Church varies from group to group. Most, however, understand the new righteousness as being based upon the love of God in Christ. This love leads to the kind of righteousness envisaged, for example, by the Beatitudes (Matthew 5:1-11); by Christ's statements about the nature of God's judgement (Matthew 25:31-46); by Christ's assertion in defense of his own conduct that the Sabbath was made for human beings, not human beings for the Sabbath (Matthew 12); and by his exposition of the covenant law (Matthew 5:17-48). This understanding of God's love introduced an element of human freedom to deal with the ambiguities, paradoxes, and inconsistencies of life, which the law can deal with only by casuistry—itself an admission of inadequacy. What the law in and of itself asserts as righteous can be affirmed, ignored, or even contradicted by what God's love in Christ requires. As Paul says, Christians are to obey the law, but they are not slaves to it. How this tension is worked out in social settings is determined, according to Paul, by the love of God that makes all people responsible for the welfare of their neighbors as commanded by Jesus Christ (Matthew 22:34-40; 5:43-48).

The life and ministry of Christ also introduces into the Christian understanding of righteousness the element of vicarious suffering and self-sacrifice. Righteousness is not based upon enlightened self-interest. Rather, it is the rejection of self-interest on behalf of one's neighbor, even if that rejection leads to suffering and death. Altruism is thus an essential ingredient of justice. Furthermore, following Christ's example of vicarious suffering, Christians may endure punishment or suffering for actions and events they are not personally responsible for. Therefore, Christians ultimately find the norms for understanding the kind of conduct or behavior that will produce and result in righteousness in

God's revelation of himself and his will in Jesus Christ, whose life and work definitively interpreted the older covenant traditions—an interpretation so different that Christians often speak of it as the new covenant or, indeed, a new righteousness.

A third belief that Christians have about the nature of justice is that any understanding of it as a gift from God cannot be separated from an understanding of human sin, or the desire of all people to usurp and pervert the authority and power of God in the pursuit of their own ends. For Christians, justice must always be viewed from a perspective that takes into account the human tendency to reject God and "make the greater cause serve them." Christians call this tendency sin. Although human beings were created for doing what is right, their rejection of God causes them to go astray. Thus, Christians view human behavior with a skepticism. As Paul says in his discussion of the importance of law for Christians, "the good that I would do is what I do not, and that which I would not do, is what I do" (paraphrasing Romans 7:13–25). Therefore, doing right, when translated into human behavior and norms for communal life, is inevitably distorted and perverted by the human inclination to do wrong.

Any Christian effort to incorporate the divine commands and patterns into human society always involves the exercise of human judgment and interpretation. How human beings perform this act depends on not only what they know of the divine revelation but also what they are—human beings whose values and ideologies have been influenced by the societies in which they live. What people know and what they do are not necessarily the same thing, and this divergence is caused by human sin. A society's desire for a just life has to take this problem into account. Often, the very people who know the law are the ones who pervert it for their own ends. Thus, God's justice cannot be equated with the justice that human beings establish for themselves, their societies, and their governments, even when these structures have been created by people who are consciously attempting to actualize God's righteousness within them.

A second implication of the impact of human sin on the achievement of justice concerns the exercise of human freedom and responsibility in implementing divine norms. Christians see that life is more likely to be faithful to the righteousness of God when its social institutions and structures embody principles and norms that lie somewhere between the extremes of legalism, totalitarianism, and absolutism and antinomianism, anarchy, and relativism. In this way, human sin can be curtailed and controlled and whatever we know of human freedom and responsibility can be balanced and realized with a minimum of social distortion.

Finally, because of human sin, Christians believe that righteousness becomes a human possibility only when human beings commit themselves wholly and fully to God's saving act in Christ. This is a belief in which, of course, neither Jews nor Muslims will concur because it is distinctly Christian. Through an act of faith in what God has done in Christ, the sinful condition of the human race, as characterized by Paul's observation, can be overcome. Neither human effort nor reliance upon the human capacity to do good can generate this possibility. If such were the case, then righteousness would not be dependent upon the grace of God but upon what human beings are able to achieve without God. This statement of Christian belief is often received as doctrinaire (and therefore often unmentioned by Christians engaged in interfaith discussions). Nevertheless, to ignore it is academically indefensible and leads to a misunderstanding of the Christian concept of justice.

This belief about human sin and its redemption in Christ is hardly a secular approach. For Christians, however, it is a crucial part of any discussion of justice as a character of human society. Indeed, it is the precondition for all concern about God and God's righteousness and their significance for human well-being. From a phenomenological point of view, this belief is no different from the Muslim belief in the Quran and the derivative *Shari'ah* as definitive interpretations of God's justice. Nor is it different from the Judaic reliance upon Talmudic norms for doing what God considers to be just.

The Practice of Justice

Implementing this understanding of justice within the life of the individual and the community is a major problem for Christians. While the revelation of God's word in Christ and Scripture deals with the substance of justice, it does not prescribe the political, social, or economic structures necessary for that justice to be achieved. Nor does it allow for absolutizing any human interpretation of a particular commandment of God into an irrevocable legal tradition. In a sense this was no problem for the New Testament Church because it lived with the expectation of

Christ's imminent return to establish the kingdom of God. At that time these difficulties would be resolved by Christ himself. The purpose of Christian life was to prepare for this immediate return.

As time passed, the return of Christ seemed less imminent; and Christians came into conflict with the governing authorities. To maintain their life and worship, Christians began to institutionalize their theological understanding of themselves as the body of Christ, adapting various ideas of governance and structure derived from the cultural traditions of the world. In this way, the establishment of the justice required by God became the responsibility not only of the individual Christian but also of these new institutional forms and processes: that is, the institutional Church.

Throughout the course of this development, both individual Christians and the Church followed the injunctions of Paul (mentioned at the beginning of this section) and obeyed and supported the law of the governing powers except when it violated what they felt to be the witness of faith that God required. In the latter case, Christians openly disobeyed and suffered the consequences. When the Church achieved a measure of political and economic strength, it sought to use its influence to bring the law of the land into conformity with the Church's understanding and practice of justice.

None of these developments took place without conflict, both within the Church when Christians differed among themselves, and within society whenever the Church's allegiance to God was pitted against the demands of the state for ultimate allegiance. Christians thus adhered to the law of the land and worked diligently to make that law conform to their understanding of the righteousness of God. Their loyalty to the law, however, was never an ultimate loyalty lest the justice and allegiance required by God be compromised and the corrupting power of human self-assertion and greed be ignored. Indeed, for many Christians, the more religious a government claimed to be, the more likely it was to be using religion for its own ignoble ends. Today, this dynamic tension between loyalty to the state and loyalty to God still characterizes the relationships between Christians and the governments of the lands in which they live.

What does this mean for interfaith relationships? I suspect that we will find great commonality in our understanding of justice as its meaning becomes clear through the study and interpretation of our respective sources of divine law. We may also find commonality in our understanding of divine love. If this were not so, most nations would have found it very difficult to sign the United Nations' Declaration on Human Rights. Nevertheless, with respect to our theological understanding of the human condition, its relationship to the possibility for social justice and righteousness, and its realization in faith, we will continue to have differences. Although these differences give each group a particular religious identity, they do not allow Christians to judge themselves and their belief superior to other religious beliefs. There is no way that Christians can make judgments outside their own a priori assumptions without usurping God's prerogatives. Christians can only say, "For us, this is the way we interpret the human response to God. Because we believe our faith to be true for us, it is therefore true for all people." Jews and Muslims will say the same from within the context of their own particular beliefs. At the same time, however, Christians must be true to their own beliefs. Thus, they should recognize that all people have an equal right to respond to God in their own way.

The commonalities in the Muslim, Christian, and Jewish understandings of justice prevent relativism and nihilism; respect for our differences prevents the absolutism and totalitarianism that the assertion of one particular truth often generates. In these circumstances all people of faith can join together in a common effort to affirm the righteousness that God enjoins upon us all.

III. Justice in Islam, Judaism, and Christianity: A Comparison

Charles Adams

When talking about justice, one must consider at least two different issues. First, what does justice mean and what does it consist of? Second, what are the procedures and processes by which justice is achieved? Usually when we discuss the subject of justice, our attention is drawn to procedures rather than a strictly philosophical consideration of the concept. In my view, however, the means of achieving justice is a fundamental issue. Most of us can agree on the kind of society we would like to see; our difficulty is knowing how to attain that ideal.

In his essay on the rabbinic interpretation of justice (section 1), Rabbi Edwards discusses procedural matters, noting that Jewish law lays down rules for courts, evidence, witnesses, and so on. In other words, Jewish law includes a large body of procedural directives that show how the Judaic concept of justice may be applied. In contrast, the procedural side of justice is poorly developed in Christian and Muslim communities. For example, Islamic law is a jurist's rather than a judge's law. It has not grown out of judges' accumulated wisdom and decisions. Rather, it has been articulated by scholars who have considered authoritative texts and written down their opinions. Often, they have worked in defiance of government authorities or have isolated themselves from any connection with government institutions. Over time, the various Muslim societies have developed courts and procedural processes; but for the most part these developments have been legitimized under the rubric of *Qanun* (the law of the ruler). In other words, rulers have felt free to construct arbitrary rules, regulations, and procedures. Of the many judicial and quasijudicial institutions that have existed throughout Muslim history, only the *Qadi*'s court has a sanction in *Shari'ah;* and the jurisdiction of the court is sharply limited. I believe that the procedural side of law and its institutional framework have to be addressed. It is not enough to deal with abstract concepts of what justice may be, nor is it sufficient to elaborate on the theological basis of justice.

I would like to make several specific points about the essays in this chapter. First, most of us have heard references to North America's pluralistic, democratic society. To the epithets pluralistic and democratic we should add secular. The vast majority of North American citizens hold notions of justice that have little religious basis. Rather, they derive from certain secular and humanistic considerations. Most Western principles of justice are rational, including notions about human rights, the equality of all people, the need for the rule of law, and so on. According to the U.S. Constitution, all humans "are endowed with certain inalienable rights"; and it is the duty of society to protect those rights. It seems to me that Jews, Christians, and Muslims who are genuinely convinced that justice and righteousness are rooted in the presence of God must acknowledge that the substantive and procedural aspects of Western justice are secular and rest on rational and experiential bases.

Second, can one talk adequately about justice in terms of an individual's inwardness? When we speak about justice in the world, are we not by definition addressing ourselves to issues that concern large groups of people in society? If we cannot speak about justice in terms of the society, then Reverend Haines's equation "righteousness equals justice" may not be very helpful, particularly if one accepts the Calvinist notion that righteousness invokes concepts of sin and salvation from sin. He has addressed the question of what happens to the individual or considered the religious destiny of a single person rather than the adjustment of the problems of a society. He has not applied the idea of vicarious suffering to a society. What are the implications of vicarious suffering for remedying the injustices and inequities suffered by countless numbers of people in the world? Furthermore, what is the relevance of inward righteousness or an act of faith to the concrete social changes that may bring about more justice? I do not understand how an individualistic Christian doctrine of salvation bears on the achievement of justice.

Finally, neither Rabbi Edwards nor Reverend Haines mention reward or punishment in terms of religious teachings about the destiny of humankind. To most people, justice has something to do with sanctions: that is, punishment for doing what the law and moral equity say should not be done. I believe that this subject must be discussed if we are to deal properly with the subject of justice.

Notes

1. In its narrowest definition Torah refers to the five books of Moses; in its broadest it includes the entire body of traditional Jewish teaching. The term is better translated as "guidance" or "instruction" rather than "law."

Connecting the Ideals to Practice

Nimat Hafez Barazangi,
M. Raquibuz Zaman,
and Omar Afzal

To connect the ideals of justice in Islam to its practice, one needs to understand how interpretations and applications of the basic precepts of this religion vary in time and place. These precepts produced a civilization comprising comprehensive religious, liturgical, ethical, and jurisprudence systems (*Shari'ah*)—a civilization that thrived from the seventh through the seventeenth centuries and remained alive despite apparent dysfunction in the eighteenth and nineteenth centuries. The mere existence of this civilization shows that Islamic identity and its search for justice has never ceased.

Today, Islamic identity is reemerging as a potent force across the globe. More than a billion followers of Islam live in every corner of the world. Relating what the religion teaches and what Muslim cultures practice may shed new light on the diversity of practice and procedure within the unity of principle. If this relationship is clarified, Jews and Christians may better understand Islam and Muslims.

Many people understand that Islamic ideals and reality are intertwined. Yet today these ideals are increasingly misinterpreted. What the Western media calls an Islamic resurgence represents the West's interpretation of the Muslim polity's reaction to injustice and oppression.

Such an interpretation does not attempt to relate events to history and context and thus does not make the events a credible representation of reality. Certainly, some Muslims have practiced basic principles of Islam without grounding their practice in a knowledge of the central concept of Islam (*Tawhid*). But this does not make the teachings of the Quran and Hadith more or less meaningful or credible.

Shari'ah is the norm by which Muslims seek to administer and supervise a just order. Few scholars and laypersons realize that the Islamic concepts of justice and righteousness go beyond the codified law, the court procedures, and the five pillars. Islamic ideals are constantly interpreted by the Muslim *Faqihs* (jurisprudents) to produce realistic solutions to numerous issues. Thus, the lack of codified procedures (see chapter 3, section 3) in the Shari'ah is not a weakness in the Islamic justice system; rather, it strengthens procedural justice—an idea that becomes clear when one recognizes that Islamic social and ethical codes were intended to remain flexible to allow for changes in space and time and circumstantial variations.

Justice in Islam lies in the ability of the human individual to recognize his or her just character. According to the Quran (82:7), the individual is intended to comprehend the ideals of the Quran as they relate to the purpose of creation and divine will (6:115). The ideals guide human beings to place the highest value on justice because it is the closest to *Taqwa* (the ability to balance the limits of God with the limits of the individual and those of society) in the human vicegerency. *Al Khilafah* (vicegerency), as discussed by Barazangi (chapter 6), fulfills the purpose of creation—to appropriate God's law of nature on earth (Quran 5:8; 6:152). These ideals also suggest educational and pedagogical procedures consistent with the values of justice ("I was ordered to act justly among you" [Quran 42:15]). The ideals and the educational procedures will also help humans at least partly attain gender justice ("And if you feared that you may not do justice [among your orphan females] then [marry] one only" [Quran 4:3] and "You are never able to be fair and just as between women, even if it is your ardent desire" [4:129]). In short, the ideals inspire visions of the good and stress the role of knowledge in the human quest for the good life. The good is an attainable reality built into human morality.

What distinguishes the ideals of justice in Islam from the just state of Plato, the individual unconditional freedom of Rousseau, and the democratic progressive society of Dewey? Justice in Islam pertains to all the elements mentioned above (a just state, an individual freedom, and a democratic, progressive society) in a harmonious quest to realize God's law of nature on earth. Therefore, the traits of a just ruler are not limited to the most intelligent, as Plato suggests. The *'Adl* (a person who attains the highest level of a just character) is the person who should be a ruler, a judge, a witness, a guardian (Quran 2:282; 4:58; 5:106; 16:76; 65:2).

As the chapters in this book make clear, different assumptions about and understandings of Islamic ideals and the attainment of justice have been developed. The Quran describes how these variations in assumptions and *Nawayah* (intentions) may lead in a direction opposite from the ideal. For example, the Arabic language and the Quran use the same Arabic root of the word 'Adl ('A, da, la) to express the basic meaning of the verb *'Adala* (to make equal). When this verb is used in a different context and with some variation in *Tanwin* (diacritics), it becomes the Arabic verb *ya'dil* (making equal among nonequals), which might lead to the denial of the central concept of Islam (the affirmation of Allah as the one God) by equating Allah with other gods (Quran 7:159, 181; 6;1, 150; 27;60; see also Ayoub's distinction between *'Adil* and *'Idl* in chapter 2).

Therefore, assuming that the Islamic concept of 'Adl mirrors the Western understanding of justice does not take into account the various derivatives and meanings of the word in particular contexts. Similarly, *Hurriyyah* (freedom), *Tahrir* (liberation), *'Adalah* (equality), *Ba'th* (revival), *Intifadah* (resurgence) need to be understood within a Quranic frame of reference. In chapter 5 Tamara Sonn says, "There are a few modern needs not met by the classical model of Islam," a perception that may result from conceptual interpretations that do not consider diverse meanings in original contexts. Such interpretations may also explain why many Muslims have fallen into the trap of *Taqlid*—that is, following predecessors' interpretations of Quranic teachings and the prophetic delineation of the Quran and not considering changes in time and space. For example, a lack of attention to the authenticity of Hadith may result in misinterpreting verses or prophetic traditions and applying certain fixed rules and principles (see chapters 4 and 6).[1] It may also lead some scholars to observe that the descriptive meanings of justice in Islam do not lend themselves to analytical definitions or deal with the overall nature of the Islamic call for justice (see chapter 5).

Ali Mazrui (chapter 7), a political scientist with a universal perspective, points out that global powers and their client states often deny Muslim countries access to crucial technologies, such as nuclear technology, so that the Muslim nations remain subservient. He demonstrates that justice and fair play are often absent when Western powers deal with the Muslim nations. Mazrui's analysis, therefore, realizes the close relationship of the ideals to practice and the duality of the ideals in Western, secular conceptions of justice. Such a duality in the ideals of justice that the West has for itself and for "others" not only represents a duality in the underlying assumptions of secular rationality, disciplines, and approaches. It is also evidence that there is a need for a different framework to understanding procedural justice in Islam. Perhaps we could fulfill this need by examining the Islamic cultural identity that encompasses both religious rationality and universal assumptions of justice.

Note

1. In "Women and Political Power in Muslim Thought: Justice Denied out of Misrepresentations?" a paper presented at the symposium "Islam and the Struggle for Justice in the World Today" (Cornell University, 1987), Muhammad H. Sherif discussed the Hadith, which says, "No nation will succeed under the leadership of a woman." He argues for reanalyzing authentic Islamic traditions. In particular, he calls for analyzing the *Matn* (the content of a tradition) in its historical context and the *Isnad* (the transmissional claim of a tradition) in accordance with the reliability of the transmitters. By analyzing the above stated Hadith and explaining its weakness, Sherif concludes that the primary sources of Islamic law do not prevent women from full political participation.

Part Two

Justice:
The Reality

Chapter Four

Economic Justice in Islam, Ideals and Reality
The Cases of Malaysia, Pakistan, and Saudi Arabia

M. Raquibuz Zaman

The Islamic economic system has at least three principal goals: (1) to satisfy the basic needs of all members of the society, including children, the disabled, the elderly, and the poor; (2) to ensure economic development to meet the needs of the growing population, provide for the continued enrichment of the society, remain strong enough to defend itself from outside aggression, and maintain its cultural identity; and (3) to keep inequalities of income in check as the society grows richer and economically stronger.[1]

The Quran clearly emphasizes individual initiative in the form of management and property ownership (see, for example, 2:276–81). God is the ultimate owner of all material resources; and *Al Insan* (human beings), as God's vicegerents on Earth, are encouraged to use them properly for their legitimate needs. This share must also be spent for the common good, including assistance to the poor and the needy.[2] Thus, Muslims with enough means must pay the *Zakah* (the obligatory charitable contributions meant to sanctify ownership of wealth) levy and spend generously on charities.[3] In addition, the state, which represents the society, must do its part as the custodian of natural resources such as water, minerals, and forests. These resources must be managed for the collective good of the society. In short, Islam aims to achieve economic goals through the mutual aid and cooperation of individuals and society.

Basic Tenets of Islamic Economics

Ways of achieving economic justice and fair play can best be understood if we first examine some of the basic tenets of Islamic economics.

Private Ownership Rights and the Rights of Free Choice

The Islamic concept of private ownership of property is somewhat different from the private enterprise system of the West. Property rights are not absolute under Islam because ultimate ownership belongs to God. Individuals can own property and accumulate wealth as long as such pursuits do not keep others from making a living, and the society has preemptive rights to regulate property ownership and allocate resources for the promotion of the common good. Natural resources are not owned individually but by the society for the benefit of all.

Although they are subject to the limitations just mentioned, individuals may own and manage private property and pass it on to their heirs. But Islamic laws of inheritance impose certain restrictions on the disposal of estates that prevent Muslims from leaving out legacies at will. (I discuss further details in the next section.)

Individuals are encouraged to choose freely the means of their livelihood as long as occupational pursuits do not override public welfare. Individual rights to pursue economic activities for personal gain are superseded by the greater need to benefit society as a whole. Thus, the development of mineral resources such as petroleum, iron ore, and coal should enrich the society rather than individuals or families.

While Islam allows Muslims to choose their occupations freely, it does set certain clear guidelines. Muslims are advised to (1) fulfill their economic needs in moderation; (2) meet the needs of their families; (3) make provisions for future contingencies; (4) provide for posterity; (5) contribute generously to promote social welfare; and, most important, (6) serve the cause of God.[4] They are warned against engaging in usury and gambling; producing or distributing prohibited products such as alcoholic beverages and intoxicants (Quran 2:219); and consuming swine flesh and its by-products, blood, the flesh of dead animals and birds, and beasts of prey (Quran 2:173; 5:4).

Even though Islam permits freedom of choice in entrepreneurial decision making, it does impose some significant restrictions to ensure social and economic justice. First, the individual must not pursue a policy that is injurious to others unless justice itself demands it.[5] Thus, a merchant cannot sell even slightly tainted food if concerns exist about possible ill-effects on consumers. An entrepreneur cannot establish factories in places where they are likely to create environmental pollution, even though such actions can be highly profitable for the individual. Similarly, attempts to create monopoly or monopsony powers should be thwarted because they have injurious effects on competition and consumers. The Prophet (PBUH) emphasized that there is to be "no injury, and no inflicting of injury" and "whosoever injures, Allah will injure him and whosoever tyrannizes, Allah shall tyrannize over him."[6]

Founding a new firm in an established industry may cause some harm to existing firms, but the increased competition is likely to improve quality of products or services and reduce prices for consumers. As long as the overall benefit to society exceeds the harm, the entrepreneur should go ahead with the project: his or her self-interest coincides with the general welfare of society. This balance between benefit and injury must be maintained to ensure justice in the economic system.

When the effect of entrepreneurial decisions is uncertain, the entrepreneur can try to advance his or her personal goals only if the injurious effects on others are likely to be very small and very uncertain. There are six basic principles to follow:[7]

1. Inevitable necessity permits the forbidden. . . .
2. What is permitted out of pressing necessity must be strictly kept within the limits imposed by that necessity. . . .
3. Injury is not to be removed by another injury. . . .
4. In the face of an inevitable choice between two injurious courses of action, the least injurious shall be chosen. . . .
5. Elimination of injuries is prior to the pursuit of utilities and whenever something useful appears wedded to some injury (so that if you are to get the utility you must also admit the injury) the elimination of injury shall generally be preferred to the attainment of utility. . . .
6. Needs sometimes assume the role of inevitable necessities whether they are individual needs or social needs. . . .

These policies, as well as those concerning "no injury" (mentioned by Imam al Shatibi in *al Muwafaqat*), form the basis of entrepreneurial policies in Islam.[8]

A second basic principle of Islamic economic justice is that ends do not justify the means. Muslims are to use just means to achieve just ends in their dealings with every human being. A buyer must receive full measure for his purchases, and the seller must receive the just price agreed upon between the two parties. God urges humankind to "give measure and weight with [full] justice" (Quran 6:152), and to say, "I believe in the Book which God has sent down, and I am commanded to judge justly between you" (Quran 42:15). God condemns those who deal in fraud and give less than what is due (Quran 83:1–4).[9] The Prophet (PBUH) advised Muslims to shun all sorts of dubious transactions and those dealing with commodities not yet harvested or processed.[10] Economic justice demands that all parties are honest with each other in all dealings and that each pays or receives what is justly due, refrains from questionable transactions, and makes contractual agreements about products or services that are in hand and clearly known to each. The rights of free choice and private ownership, therefore, imply significant obligations on all Muslims to work for the common good.

The Role of the State in the Economy

The state as the representative of the society plays an active role in economic activities. It must ensure that every citizen has the opportunity to seek work and make a living. The eradication of poverty and the creation of job opportunities are primary economic functions of the state. It must ensure equitable distribution of wealth and initiate economic growth and development. It has the responsibility to maintain price stability and promote the economic welfare of all its people.[11]

As the custodian of all natural resources, the state must make sure that the benefits derived from them are shared by all. The state does not necessarily have to develop and manage natural resources; private enterprises can expand mineral resources or manufacture forest products if operational efficiency demands it. Nevertheless, the profits from such ventures should not be entirely pocketed by individual concerns. The state ensures that all members of the society have access to natural resources and are able to derive benefits from them.

The state has to develop the economic infrastructure that facilitates the growth of economic activities. Creation and distribution of public goods are part of its *Furud Kifayah* (collective obligatory duties).[12] Fiscally, the state is called upon to promote economic growth and development while reducing income inequalities. It should rationally allocate resources between private and public goods to promote economic efficiency and stability. It is obliged to insulate citizens from extreme economic fluctuations, especially from inflation and recessions.

The distributive function of the state calls for collection of taxes and transfer of income and resources. Taxing the spurious consumption of the rich to finance subsidies for the poor is one measure the state can resort to. By financing education and training for the poor and reallocating some state-owned properties to them, the state can facilitate redistribution of income in the economy. It can engage in economic development programs and projects to create job opportunities for the poor and growth of income for all. To facilitate the growth of private enterprise, the state can allocate resources to subsidies, price supports, and technical policies and resort to tax concessions and other forms of incentives. One of the duties of the Islamic state is to create and maintain an efficient social security system that can take care of the disabled, the indigent, and the elderly—perhaps using funds from the Zakah levy and charitable donations. Because the state has the authority to tax its citizens and control natural resources, it should be able to generate the funds to accomplish the tasks that Islam entrusts to it.

Prevention of fraud and illegal transactions are other important responsibilities of the state. To monitor transactions, check weights and measures, and ensure the smooth operation of the market system, Islam introduced the institution of *Hisba*. The duty of the *Muhtasib* is to promote and enforce spiritual and ethical values in every aspect of life. Periodically, the Muhtasib checks weights and measures for accuracy, examines business transactions to ensure absence of fraud and deceit, and prevents illegal contracts such as *Muʿamalat Ribawiyah* (usurious transactions), *Bayʿ al Gharar* (speculative sales), and *Najsh* (bidding up of prices without intention to purchase). The Muhtasib is also responsible for ensuring that business communities do not hoard or manipulate supplies to bid up prices.[13] Early Islamic states had similar responsibilities: regulating business, setting up markets, protecting trade routes, creating communication facilities, establishing free ration depots, and granting loans to traders and entrepreneurs.[14]

The Prohibition of Riba

The prohibition of *Riba* (usury) is one of the key features of Islamic economic justice because it clearly prevents the rich and greedy from exploiting the poor. The Quran repeatedly exhorts Muslims to stay away from usury: "O ye who believe! Fear God, and give up what remains of your demand for usury, if ye are indeed believers" (2:278).[15]

Riba in Islam means excess or increase over the amount lent. Any predetermined amount over the principal is considered usurious. *Riba al Fadl,* which is excess over quantities (for transactions in kind), is strictly forbidden. Thus, if someone borrows a particular item, the debtor must return the same item of the same kind.[16] Exchanges of gold for silver or dried fruit for fresh are considered usurious transactions. Similarly, *Riba Nasiá* (fixed charges on money loans) are also prohibited. The creditor should not earn an excess amount from the principal lent to the borrower.

There are some questions about charging higher prices for items sold on credit.[17] In general, Muslim jurists feel that such transactions should be avoided unless there is reason to believe that higher prices for deferred payment are justified on grounds of equity.[18]

Ways of Promoting Economic Justice

An Islamic society must uphold the *Shari'ah,* whose basic objective is to promote *Maslahah* (public interest or welfare). Therefore, Islam urges individuals to cooperate with each other and the state in promoting mutual aid and trust for the economic betterment of all. This section discusses some basic institutions that are directly responsible for promoting economic justice.

Al Zakah

Al Zakah (a levy to purify wealth) is one of the five basic pillars of Islam.[19] Anyone who has enough money to meet the basic necessities and comforts of life possesses *Nisab* (leviable wealth).[20] Therefore, these people should pay Zakah, which should be used exclusively for supporting *al Fuqara* (the poor), *al Masakin* (the needy), *al 'Amelin 'Alaiha* (the administrators of Zakah), *al Muállafatu qulubuhum* (those whose hearts have been reconciled to Islam), *Wa Fil Riqab* (for the ransoming of slaves), *al Gharemin* (debtors), *Wa Fi Sabil Allah* (in the cause of God), *Wa ibn al Sabil* (and for the wayfarer) (Quran 9:60). The state is primarily responsible for assessing and collecting Zakah and distributing its proceeds among the intended recipients.[21] Zakah is levied on all legal sources of income from various economic sectors and all idle savings in cash and kind (for example, precious metals).[22]

The proceeds from Zakah collection can go a long way toward meeting the financial needs of the poor and disadvantaged. During the first few centuries of Islam Muslim rulers occasionally had trouble finding people who needed Zakah funds. When possible, the money is sufficient to cover a recipient's living expenses for a year. The institution not only makes it possible to redistribute surplus income but also allows many recipients to become economically self-sufficient. Later they, too, will join the ranks of those who pay Zakah. I should note here that Zakah is often paid in kind rather than cash. For example, a farmer without draft animals to plow his land may receive those animals as Zakah, thus making him self-sufficient.

Voluntary Charities

The Zakah levy is compulsory for those who possess Nisab; but God urges all Muslims, rich or poor, to give generously in charity from whatever wealth He has bestowed on them. This voluntary charity is known as *Al Sadaqah*. According to the Quran, "they ask you how much they are to spend [in charity]; Say: What is beyond your need" (2:219). Muslims are urged to give anything in excess of their reasonable needs as *Infaq al 'Afw* (charity for righteousness and forgiveness).[23] "By no means shall ye attain righteousness unless ye spend [in charity] of that which ye love; and whatever ye give, of a truth God knoweth it well" (Quran 3:92).[24]

By urging Muslims to give generously in charity, Islam reminds them of their obligation to God, who is the ultimate owner and source of all resources. He is most pleased when individuals are willing to share their good fortune with those who do not. Thus, Muslims are morally obliged to use their wealth for themselves and their families and to help those less fortunate. If everyone followed the teachings of Islam with respect to Sadaqah, Zakah, and the principles of mutual aid, severe income inequalities would not exist in an Islamic society.

Waqf (religious endowment) is another form of voluntary charity that has significantly enhanced public welfare. Individuals with wealth may leave a portion of their holdings in Waqf, which is administered by the state or a government agency for the benefit of intended recipients. One advantage of the Waqf system is that it is a continuous charity: the donor does not personally have to look for suitable recipients. Throughout Islamic history Waqf properties have been used to run orphanages, hospitals, educational institutions, mosques and religious centers, guest houses for weary travelers, and so on.[25] In some ways the modern philanthropic foundations of the West resemble the institution of Waqf in Islam.

There are a number of other religious rites, such as the sacrifice of animals on *'Id al Adha* (the feast of immolation) and *Kaffarah* (expiation and atonement), that allow an individual to atone for violating obligatory duties, taking unlawful oaths, or exhibiting moral turpitude. These institutions also benefit the needy. On 'Id al Adha, part of the sacrificed meat is distributed to the poor. Similarly, Kaffarah often calls for feeding the poor, clothing them, or freeing those in bondage.[26]

In their *Wasiyah* (will), Muslims are allowed to leave up to one-third of their estate to be spent in charities to nonrelated poor. (Close relatives share in the deceased person's property.) Part of such legacies may be set up as a Waqf property.

Various Islamic laws that concern mutual support and cooperation are meant to promote economic justice. *Al Musa'adah* (the law of mutual aid) entitles an indebted person to seek the assistance of other Muslims in paying off the creditor if he or she cannot meet the due date. *Bait al Mal* (the public treasury) may pay off such a debt from its Zakah funds if the creditor does not remit the debt (which Islam encourages if the debtor is in straitened circumstances). The *Diyah* (blood money) that a person has to pay for accidentally killing another person is raised among family members and from personal resources. According to Islamic laws of inheritance, because family members inherit a person's wealth, they must share his hardships and good fortune equally. Similarly, a wayfarer stranded abroad must be helped out by local Muslims even if he or she is a rich person at home.[27]

Al Diyafah (the law of hospitality) makes it a social obligation to treat guests graciously. The traditions of the Prophet (PBUH) are quite clear on this issue: "He who believes in God and the last day must honor his guest for one day and one night as well as granting him hospitality for three days. More than this is considered *Sadaqh*. A guest, then, should not stay longer in order that he might not embarrass his host."[28]

Al Musharakah (the law of sharing) obligates Muslims to share their harvest of crops with those who cannot afford to buy them. Similarly, when the time comes for inheritors to divide the property of the deceased, believers are urged not to forget the poor and the orphans present at the time of division: "But if at the time of division, other relatives, or orphans, or poor are present, feed them out of the property and speak to them words of kindness and justice" (Quran 4:8).

Al Ma'un (the law of acting in kindness) requires Muslims not only to give generously to charities, but also to lend useful tools and equipment to needy neighbors: "So woe to the worshippers who are neglectful of their prayers, those who [want only] to be seen [by men], but refuse [to supply even] neighborly needs" (Quran 107:4–7). Exchanging household implements not only saves someone from suffering, but also promotes mutual understanding and fellow feeling.

Al Írth

Al Írth (the Islamic laws of inheritance) promote economic justice and equality by distributing an estate among all members of the family, including distant relatives or neighbors present at the time of division. In chapter 4 of the Quran, entitled *Al Nisaá* (The Women), God lays down the basic principles of dividing an estate. Verses 11 and 12 are particularly pertinent:

> God [thus] directs you as regards your children's [inheritance]; to the male a portion equal to that of two females: if only daughters, two or more, their share is two-thirds of the inheritance; if only one, her share is a half. For parents, a sixth share of the inheritance to each, if the deceased left children; if no children, and the parents are the [only] heirs, the mother has a third; if the deceased left brothers [or sisters] the mother has a sixth. [The distribution in all cases is] after the payment of legacies and debts. Ye know not whether your parents or your children are nearest to you in benefit. These are settled portions ordained by God; and God is All-Knowing, All-Wise.
>
> In what your wives leave, your share is a half, if they leave no child; but if they leave a child, ye get a fourth; after payment of legacies and debts. In what ye leave, their share is a fourth, if ye leave no child; but if ye leave a child, they get an eighth; after payment of legacies and debts.
>
> If the man or woman whose inheritance is in question has left

neither ascendants nor descendants, but has left a brother or a sister, each one of the two gets a sixth; but if more than two, they share in a third; after payment of legacies and debts; so that no loss is caused [to anyone]. Thus it is ordained by God; and God is All-Knowing, most Forebearing.

These verses, as well as others, and their interpretations and the related sayings of the Prophet (PBUH) clearly indicate that Islam abhors concentration of wealth in the hands of a few and urges believers to share their wealth.

The Pursuit of Economic Justice in Modern Muslim States

The various Islamic ways of promoting economic justice function well only if citizens and administrators of the state adhere to Islamic teachings in spirit and action. Let us now examine the economic policies of three Muslim states (one of which claims to be an Islamic republic) to get some idea about the implementation of these lofty ideals. A number of Muslim countries claim to be Islamic states, yet in reality few nations comprehensively observe Shari'ah (Islamic jurisprudence). In this section I examine Malaysia, Pakistan, and Saudi Arabia to ascertain if one government is better than the others at finding divine solutions for economic problems.

Malaysia

Malaysia is a federation of states with a constitutional monarchy. Political power lies in the hands of the elected prime minister and a parliament consisting of two bodies: *Dewan Negara* (the Senate) and *Dewan Ra'ayat* (the House of Representatives). Although the country has a sizable non-Muslim population, the majority of voters are Muslims.[29] Malaysia is the most democratic of the fifty or so Muslim countries in the world. It has three main ethnic groups: Malay (44 percent), Chinese (36 percent), and Indian subcontinent (10 percent).

Unlike most Muslim states, Malaysia puts some Islamic economic institutions into practice. Because religious matters are under the jurisdiction of state authorities, the collection and distribution of Zakah are the responsibility of the state governments.[30] Economic planning and development projects, however, are in the hands of the federal government, whose activities reflect the Western secular tradition. The Malaysian constitution proclaims that Islam is the state religion. Yet for the most part, adherence to Shari'ah and Islamic economic precepts is limited to Muslims within individual states.[31]

The Malaysian states do collect *Zakat al 'Ushr*, a 10-percent levy on agricultural produce. (Malaysians often refer to Zakah as 'Ushr.) This collection comes primarily from rice farmers, 88 percent of whom lived below the poverty line in 1970. Thus, the burden of Zakah is borne essentially by those in the lower part of the economic spectrum.[32] From the administrative point of view, 'Ushr is the easiest Zakah to collect; it is rarely collected from business, commerce, industry, and urban wage earners. As a result, there are not enough Zakah funds to eradicate poverty. (I should note here that the rice farmers pay income taxes without receiving credit for the Zakah levy because of lack of coordination between the local Zakah administration and centrally directed tax collectors.)[33]

Because resources for economic development and planning are administered by the federal government, it alone can take a decisive step toward establishing economic justice. The Malaysian development philosophy is based on the *Rukun Negara* (national ideology), which was conceived in 1969 after a racial crisis. Interestingly, one of the five principles under Rukun Negara is the creation of "a just society in which the wealth of the nation shall be equitably shared."[34] Moreover, a guiding principle in the implementation of this ideology is a belief in God.

It is quite clear that Malaysia has been trying to achieve Islamic goals implicitly through its development plans and governmental resource allocations. The nation claims that the number of Malaysians living at the poverty level declined to below 15 percent in rural areas and 4.5 percent in urban areas in 1990, compared to 44.8 percent and 21.8 percent, respectively, in 1973. The government plans to eliminate it altogether by the year 2000.[35]

For a country with its economic means, Malaysia has a reasonable social security system. Old age, disability, death, sickness, maternity, and work injury are covered to a limited extent by individual employers who cooperate with the government.[36] Nevertheless, the country needs to do much more. At present, there are no unemployment or family allowances. As Malaysia's economic base strengthens and it begins to implement Islamic institutions throughout the country, the nation may yet achieve its goal of becoming a just society with an equitable distribution of wealth.

Pakistan

The Islamic republic of Pakistan has a population of about one hundred and twenty million, of which 97 percent are Muslims.[37] Pakistan has been under military rule for most of its forty-year existence. Since the 1988 election, Pakistan has embarked on a parliamentary form of democracy. From 1977 to 1987, the military government attempted to introduce Islamic reforms at a gradual pace, "promulgat[ing] the *Zakat* and *'Ushr* Ordinance on June 20, 1980. While *Zakat* collection was enacted from the date of the Ordinance, because of administrative difficulties, *'Ushr* collection was enacted only from 15th March 1983."[38]

Pakistan made progress with Zakah during the military regime of Zia-ul-Haq. In 1980–81, it collected about 844 million rupees, and by 1984–85 the collection rose to 1.2 billion rupees.[39] Even though these sums equaled a fraction of the total tax revenue of the government, they were nonetheless impressive. The 'Ushr proceeds represented about 0.2 percent of the total value in the crop subsector. Pakistan used part of the Zakah proceeds to pay for the education of its poorest students, and the National Zakat Foundation financed some projects here and there.

As of July 1985, Pakistan stopped interest-bearing deposits in its banks. Since 1981 it has been introducing bank reforms to meet Islamic principles concerning usury (Riba). Pakistan's Participation Term Certificates (PTCs), Profit-Loss Sharing Accounts (PLS), *Mudarabah* Certificates (partnership certificates in commercial ventures), and the abolition of interest-bearing accounts seemed to be in line with the requirements of Shari'ah. In reality, however, bankers continued their old ways of doing business, using Islamic terms as a cover but achieving the same profits.[40]

> In sum the government appeared to have succeeded in creating the possibility of a fully Islamic system of commerce and finance, without any major disruption of economic activity. . . . While efforts must continue to align the system further to Islam by eliminating prohibited transactions, the speed with which this can be done will depend largely on the speed with which depositors,

banks, and their borrowers voluntarily move towards those sanctioned practices that meet the approval of the *'Ulema* [religious scholars], and of Allah."⁴¹

Pakistan claims that its distribution of income favorably compares with developed countries such as France, Great Britain, and the United States in terms of the percentage share of the poorest 40 percent of the population.⁴² Recent estimates show, however, that concentration of wealth among the rich has increased at the cost of the poor.⁴³

Pakistan, like Malaysia, has instituted a modest social security system.⁴⁴ Even though it does not cover every Pakistani, it nonetheless represents a significant step toward economic justice in this poor country.

Saudi Arabia

"The Kingdom of Saudi Arabia is almost the only country among the Arab and Islamic States whose Constitution is the Holy Quran and the principles of the Prophet's [PBUH] *Sunnah.*" Thus states the *Third Development Plan: 1400–1405 A.H.—1980–1985 A.D.*⁴⁵ According to the plan, development policies are "to maintain the religious and moral values of Islam, and to assure the defense of religion and country."

The government of the Kingdom of Saudi Arabia stopped collecting Zakah in the mid-1970s when its oil revenue began to rise dramatically. Instead, Zakah distribution is now the responsibility of the individual payer. In other words, this great obligatory institution of Islam has been relegated to a purely voluntary religious duty for practicing Muslims. Although a great many wealthy Saudis do pay Zakah, it is not clear how well the money is distributed among categories of recipients.

The enormous oil wealth of Saudi Arabia has made it possible for the kingdom to launch a social security system for its citizens.⁴⁶ In 1962, the benefits equaled Saudi riyal (SR) 360 for the head of the household and SR 120 for each dependent, with a total of up to SR 1,540 per family. By 1986 these benefits rose to SR 2,268, SR 1,512, and SR 11,340, respectively.⁴⁷ The Saudi government has spent large sums of money to help its citizens build houses, pay for education and training, and subsidize basic consumer goods and services. One could argue that poor Saudi citizens are better off today than many members of the lower middle classes in the both developed and developing countries.

Now the government must further its implementation of the Islamic system of economic justice to be more generous to noncitizens who are long-term residents of the country.

Shari'ah laws are not strictly followed in the Saudi financial system. Officially, dealing in interest is not recognized; but most bank lending and borrowing are based on fixed charges and fees (an indirect name for interest). The declining oil prices of 1985–86 slowed the tempo of economic activities, making many large private debtors more conscious about Shari'ah injunctions against dealing with interest. At the insistence of the Saudi Arabian Monetary Agency (SAMA), Al Rajhi, the largest Saudi company involved in currency exchange and commerce, decided to become an Islamic bank by the end of 1986.[48]

Islam emphasizes economic justice and fair play. It does not call for the same distribution of wealth and income to all, but it does want the poor have enough to meet the basic necessities of life.[49] Both individual members of society and the state must strive for economic justice.

Today, implementation of the Islamic system of economic justice is still in its infancy. After a long period of colonial domination, most Muslim countries are now beginning to see that the Western and Eastern economic systems are not entirely successful in alleviating economic problems. Within the last few decades, countries such as Malaysia, Pakistan, and Saudi Arabia have begun to adopt Islamic economic practices; and the results are quite encouraging. Once the process of Islamization begins in earnest, it is bound to lead to better distribution of income and wealth among citizens.

Notes

1. For details, see S. M. Yusuf, *Economic Justice in Islam* (Lahore, Pakistan: Sh. Muhammad Ashraf, 1971), chap. 1; and M. N. Siddiqi, "Some Notes on Teaching Economics in Islamic Perspective: Public Finance" (Unpublished MS, Centre for Research in Islamic Economics, King Abdulaziz University, Jeddah, Saudi Arabia, 1986), 9.

2. Verses of the Quran dealing with this subject include 1:78; 2:2–7; 7:1–3; 20:6; 32:9; and 57:7. For a detailed analysis, see H. Askari, *Society and State in Islam: An Introduction* (New Delhi: Islam and the Modern Age Society, 1978), chap. 4.

3. Relevant Quranic verses include 2:43, 83, 110, 177, 277; 4:77, 162; 5:13, 58; 7:156; 9:11, 18, 60, 71; 19:55; 22:78; 30:39.

4. For details, see M. N. Siddiqi, *The Economic Enterprise in Islam* (Lahore, Pakistan: Islamic Publications, 1972), chap. 1.

5. For a detailed exposition on this issue, see Siddiqi, "Some Notes," 42–52.

6. Quoted from al Bukhari by Siddiqi, "Some Notes," 43; the Hadith narrated by Ibn Hurirah and quoted by Siddiqi, "Some Notes," 43.

7. Quoted from Ibn-Nujaym's *Al Áshbah wal-al Nadhair* by Siddiqi, *Economic Enterprise*, 50–51.

8. See Siddiqi, "Some Notes," 44–50.

9. There are many other verses in the Quran on this subject. For example, see 17:35; 7:8–9, 85; 11:84–85; 55:8–9; 57:25.

10. Dubious transactions involve selecting the commodity randomly by throwing a stone or touching it rather than properly inspecting it. See Siddiqi, *Economic Enterprise*, chap. 1, for references. There are a number of prophetic traditions on the subject of unprocessed commodities. See, for example, al Bukhari, "Chapter on the Book of Al-Salam," vol. 3 of *Sahih al-Bukhari*, trans. Muhammad Mohsin Khan (Ankara, Turkey: Hilal Yayinlari, 1976), 243–49.

11. The principal responsibility of the state is, of course, to maintain law and order, build an effective national defense, develop harmonious relations with other nations, and promote social and economic justice. For details, see M. Umar Chapra, "The Islamic Welfare State and Its Role in the Economy," in *Studies in Islamic Economics*, ed. Kurshid Ahmed (Leicester, U.K.: Islamic Foundation, 1980), 143–69.

12. For an elaborate discussion of this topic, see Siddiqi, "Some Notes."

13. For a detailed analysis of the institution of Hisba, see Ibn Taymiya, *Public Duties in Islam: The Institution of the Hisba*, translated by Muhtar Holland (Leicester, U.K.: Islamic Foundation, 1982).

14. For an excellent exposition on the economic activities of early Islamic states, see S. M. Hasan-uz-Zaman, *The Economic Functions of the Early Islamic State*, (Karachi, Pakistan: International Publishers, 1981).

15. Other Quranic verses are 2:275; 3:130; 4:161; and 30:39.

16. For details on the question of usury, see Afzal-ur-Rahman, *Economic Doctrines of Islam*, vol. 3 (Lahore, Pakistan: Islamic Publications, 1976), chap. 5; and Y. Al Qardawi, *The Lawful and the Prohibited in Islam*, translated by K. el Hebawy, M. M. Siddiqui, and S. Shukry (Indianapolis: American Trust Publications, 1980), 264–70.

17. See M. Abu-Saud, *Contemporary Economic Issues: Usury and Interest*, (Cincinnati, Ohio: Zakat and Research Foundation, 1986), 12–17. See also Ibn Malik, *Muwatta*, translated by M. Rahimuddin (Lahore, Pakistan: Sh. Muhammad Ashraf, 1985), chaps. 402–4.

18. See Abu-Saud, *Contemporary Economic Issues*, 17.

19. The five pillars are (1) believe in the oneness of God and that Muhammad (PBUH) is a messenger of God; (2) pray five times daily; (3) pay Zakah for whom it is due; (4) fast in the month of Ramadhan; and (5) make a pilgrimage to Mecca if you can afford to do so.

20. For the estimation of Nisab for various income groups see A. A. Shaik,

"Concept of *Zakah*: A Survey of Quranic Texts and Their Explanations in Shariah and Contemporary Economics," in *Some Aspects of the Economics of Zakah*, edited by M. R. Zaman (Indianapolis: American Trust Publications, 1981), chap. 1; and M. R. Zaman, *Some Administrative Aspects of the Collection and Distribution of Zakah and the Distributive Effects of the Introduction of Zakah into Modern Economics* (Jeddah, Saudi Arabia: Scientific Publishing Centre, King Abdulaziz University, 1987).

21. Until the time of the third caliph, 'Uthman, Zakah was collected and distributed by the state. The Prophet (PBUH) introduced this practice himself. 'Uthman, however, changed this practice by delegating the authority of distribution to Zakah payers themselves. For details on this issue, see N. P. Aghnides, *Mohammedan Theories of Finance* (Lahore, Pakistan: Premier Book House, n.d.), chaps. 3 and 9.

22. For various rates of Zakah levy, see Zaman, *Some Administrative Aspects*, notes for chap. 4.

23. There are many verses from the Quran that urge believers to spend generously on charity, including 2:2, 215, 219, 262, 265; 4:38; 28:54; 32:16; 42:38; 57:10; and 63:10.

24. The Prophet (PBUH) repeatedly urged Muslims to practice regular charity along with prayers. The Hadith can be found, among other sources, in al Bukhari, "Kitab Al Zakah," *Sahih al Bukhari*.

25. To quote Y. Al Qaradawi, *Economic Security in Islam*, translated by M. I. Siddiqi (Lahore, Pakistan: Kazi Publications, 1981), 173: "There was no period or a phase of man's life for which a *Waqf* was not created by the affluent people of the Muslim society. These *Awqaf*, wide and varied, were a source of great honor for the administration of orphanages, etc., which were set up to meet the need for the orphans for their food and lodging, medical treatment, etc."

26. "God will not call you to account for what is futile in your oaths, but He will call you to account for your deliberate oaths: for expiation, feed ten indigent persons on a scale of the average for the food of your families; or clothe them, or give a slave his freedom. If that is beyond your means, fast for three days. This is the expiation for the oath you have sworn" (Quran 5:89).

27. For details, see N. B. Taib, "Islam and Eradication of Poverty" (Ph.D. diss., Temple University, Philadelphia, 1988), chap. 5.

28. Al Bukhari, *Sahih al-Bukhari*, vol. 3, chap. 31.

29. These percentages were collected from *Reader's Digest Almanac of 1987*, (Pleasantville, N.Y.: Reader's Digest Association, 1987), 610. See also *Asia 1987 Yearbook* (Hong Kong: Far Eastern Economic Review, 1987), 185–91.

30. For a critical analysis of the Malaysia's limited Zakah system, see I. M. Saleh and R. Ngah, "Distribution of *Zakah* Burden on Padi Producers in Malaysia," in Zaman, *Some Aspects of the Economics of Zakah*, 80–153.

31. For a detailed analysis of Malaysian development plans and their impact on economic justice, see M. S. Sidek, "Islam and Development: An Ethical Analysis with Special Emphasis on Public Resource Utilization in Malaysia." (Ph.D. diss., Temple University, Philadelphia, 1987), chap. 4.

32. Saleh and Ngah, "Distribution of *Zakah* Burden," 82.

33. Ibid., 115.

34. Sidek, "Islam and Development," 8. Quoted from Government of Malaysia, *Rukun Negara* (Kuala Lumpur: Government Printer, 1971).

35. These data are cited from the *Trends in Developing Economies 1993* (Washington, D.C.: World Bank, 1993), 307.

36. For details, see U.S. Department of Health and Human Services, *Social Security Programs Throughout the World—1983* (Washington, D.C.: Social Security Administration, Office of Policy, Research Report No. 59, April 1984), 160–61, 248–49.

37. *World Development Report 1994* (Washington, D.C. World Bank, 1994), 162.

38. Islamic Republic of Pakistan. *Economic Survey: 1984–85* (Islamabad: Ministry of Finance, 1985), 13.

39. For sources of data, see Pakistan, *Economic Survey*, tables 3 and 14.

40. Pakistan's *Economic Survey*, 11–13, is very candid about progress.

41. Ibid., 13.

42. Pakistan, *Economic Survey*, xiv.

43. World Bank, *Social Indicators of Development 1993* (Washington, D.C.: World Bank, 1993), 255.

44. See U.S. Department of Health and Human Services, *Social Security Programs*, 190–91.

45. Ministry of Planning, Saudi Arabia, *The Third Development Plan: 1400–1405 A.H.—1980–1985 A.D.* (1400 A.H.), sec. 6.6.1.1, p. 385.

46. See U.S. Department of Health and Human Services, *Social Security Programs* (1983), 214–15; (1993), 283–84.

47. These data are quoted from A. Mackie, "Saudi Arabia," *Middle East Review, 1986,* 3 (June 1986): 2.

48. Ibid., 183–85.

49. "It is we who portion out between them their livelihood in the life of this world: and we raise some of them above others in ranks, so that some may command work for others" (Quran 43:32). "It is He who has made you [His] agents, inheritors of the earth: He has raised you in ranks, some above the others: that He may try you in the gifts He has given you" (Quran 6:165).

Chapter Five

The Islamic Call
Social Justice and Political Realism

Tamara Sonn

Like Judaism and Christianity, Islam calls for universal social justice. But uniquely among the monotheistic traditions, Islam makes this call its primary task. God's will for humanity is that the equality of all before God be reflected in the socioeconomic order. The Islamic imperative is submission to God's will, and God's revealed will is that we create a just society. Judaism and Christianity began in righteousness; but, according to Islam, both religions somehow lost sight of this primary goal. The Jews placed too much emphasis on the exclusivity of their task, and the Christians placed too much emphasis on Jesus' ability to achieve human salvation. Both gave too little emphasis on individual responsibility to contribute to a just society as the means to salvation. This was why the Prophet Muhammad (PBUH) was sent: to correct these aberrations and set forth in specific terms the call for universal social justice.

This emphasis on Islam as a call for social justice—*al Da'wah* (often abbreviated as "the Call")—is a relatively recent phenomenon. It is the dominant feature of what is variously called the *Nahdah* (progress, revival), Islamic resurgence, Islamic fundamentalism, and so on. By whatever name, it is at once an accurate reflection of the uniqueness of Islam and a response to specific sociopolitical realities facing the Muslim world.

If the call for universal social justice is really the identifying characteristic of Islam, why has the Islamic community waited until now to tell the world about it? What in the current context has brought this call to the forefront of Muslim consciousness? I believe the answers to these questions reveal a pattern among the many formulations of the current call for social justice. Most are little more than echoes of past political glories, anachronisms with no prescriptive power. Some, however, clearly consider not only Islamic ideals but current realities. They represent advances in the development of Islamic thought and, as such, point to its future path.

Like the ethical structure of Judaism, Islamic ethical structure differs from the Christian model because it concerns social ethics.[1] Christianity tends to approach ethics primarily on the individual level and treats social ethics as a kind of macro-ethics. For Christians, the goal of ethical behavior is personal salvation—a positive disposition in the afterlife. In Judaism and Islam, on the other hand, the principal consideration is life on earth. Ethical behavior contributes to the creation of a just society, which is God's kingdom on earth. That is the only standard of measurement of people's behavior. The Quran says that the Muslim community was created to be a just society.[2] It is to "guide by the truth and by it act with justice."[3] Its purpose is to enjoin good and prevent evil (Quran 3:110). Goodness is always measured in terms of social justice: honesty, fairness in business matters, equality of women, and so on.

Because of its social nature, Islamic ethics has generally been ensconced in Islamic law rather than ethical discourses.[4] As Fazlur Rahman characterizes it, "[Islamic law] is not strictly speaking law, since much of it embodies moral and quasi-moral precepts not enforceable in any court. Further, Islamic law, though a certain part of it came to be enforced almost uniformly throughout the Muslim world . . . is on closer examination a body of legal opinions . . . , 'an endless discussion of the duties of a Muslim,' rather than a neatly formulated code or codes."[5]

Ethics and Islamic Modernism

Only in the modern age have Muslims undertaken to articulate an ethic on the Christian model. The earliest, Sayyid Amir 'Ali's *The Ethics of Islam* (1893), responded to allegations of immorality emanating from Christianity. This and similar works attempted to scrutinize Islam from a Christian viewpoint, to show that Islam was everything Christianity was and more. They were meant primarily for Western consumption.

But history soon prompted a more inward search, born of the realization that the Muslim world had become effete in the face of foreign control and a determination to correct that condition.

The development of Islamic modernism has followed a well-known path. Its earliest representatives sought to identify the source of weakness in the Muslim world and found it in religious laxity. A common theme was that the Muslim world had slipped into stagnation by abandoning its Quranically mandated responsibility to seek knowledge in order to advance social well-being. The West had outstripped the Islamic East in science and technology, thus allowing politico-economic domination. According to this reasoning, the unyielding *'Ulema* bore most of the responsibility for this weakness. They had fostered an ethic of *Taqlid* to stifle any power-threatening initiative from the community. The early modernists therefore sought to emphasize both the Islamic call for individual initiative and the need to adapt Western learning to fit the needs of the Islamic world.

Before World War I, these efforts generally received a positive response; but their credibility was destroyed in the aftermath of the war. The West betrayed the Arabs' hope for independence and instead parceled out Arab lands to the British and the French, actions that caused a reaction against everything Western. The openness to new cultural, social, and political forms was replaced by a fierce desire to preserve the uniqueness, dignity, and self-sufficiency of Islam. Popular allegiance eventually shifted to Muslim brotherhoods that advocated little more concrete than an abiding faith in God and Islam. The continued abuses inherent in foreign occupation and the eventual displacement of millions of Arabs only served to galvanize this position.

This betrayal-response has conditioned today's popular reactionary Islam. It is a return to what Muslims perceive as a righteous and glorious past. There is a popular belief that if Islam once created the victories of the past, it can do so again. Therefore, many Muslims want to return to the system that produced that society—a system they consider total and complete and in need of almost no modification. Now as then, the term *Bid'a* (innovation) is synonymous with aberration or heterodoxy. The *Shari'ah* in all its specific formulations—legal, social, and political—is considered the tried and true path to success.

Unfortunately, however, a few modern needs are not met by the classical model of Islam. Both stem from the fact that the Shari'ah was formulated at a time when the Islamic world was politically, economically, and culturally dominant, centuries before the West had even developed its vernacular languages.[6] In this situation, the self-identity of Islam was taken for granted. Islam was the community of God; and most intellectual efforts were directed toward making it work, not defining it. Discussions of justice tended toward practical descriptions and hypothetical cases that depended on analytical induction rather than analytical definitions.[7] For example, when the *Umayyad* caliph, Abdul Malik (d. 705), asked his legists for the meaning of justice, he received the following response:

> '*Adl* [justice] may take four forms: Justice in making decisions in accordance with God's saying "When you judge among men you should judge with justice" (Quran 4:61); justice in speech in according with His saying "When you speak, you should be equitable" (Quran 6:153); justice in [the pursuit] of salvation in accordance with His saying "Protect yourselves against a day when no person will give any satisfaction instead of another, nor will an equivalent be accepted from him, nor will intercession avail him" (Quran 2:117); justice in the sense of attributing an equal to God in accordance with His saying "Yet the unbelievers attribute an equal to Him." (Quran 6:1)[8]

The passage continues to discuss justice among wives, justice in weights and measures, and so on. But nowhere does it deal with the overall nature of the Islamic call for justice. Philosophers and religious scholars followed a similar pattern. The identity of the Islamic community as one committed to justice was so ingrained into the collective consciousness that the term 'Adl (literally, median or mean), which the Quran uses to describe it, simply became a synonym for justice. Islamic hegemony was a fact of life. The purpose of the community was not a matter for debate.

In the modern age, by contrast, the Islamic world is desperately seeking a sense of identity after emerging from decades of colonial domination and centuries of political decline. During its eclipse, other communities arose to assume dominance—groups and nations with unique characteristics and ideological justifications. Edward Said's *After the Last Sky* examines this search for identity from the Palestinian viewpoint. But what he says of Arabs, I think, applies throughout the Muslim world: "We all know that we are Arabs, and yet the concept, not to say the lived actuality, of Arabism—once the creed and the discourse of a proud nation, free of imperialism, united, respected, powerful—is fast disappearing, cut up into the cautious defensiveness of relatively provincial Arab states, each with its own traditions—partly invented, partly real—each with its own nationalist and restricted identity."[9]

This search for a sense of communal identity has given rise to the modern Islamic emphasis on the Call. Muslims find comfort in past glories and hope in the Shari'ah, both of which are encompassed in the succinct, epigrammatic term "Call." The newness of its popularity in no way mitigates its authenticity, but it does reflect some historical revisionism. The call to universal social justice is nearly always couched in revolutionary terms. Its very significance derives from the lack of social justice outside the Muslim world.

Certainly, the Prophet's (PBUH) mission is often called a revolution against a decadent sociomoral situation; but the Prophet (PBUH) himself did not refer to it as such. His word rang with moral exhortation and spiritual edification. In fact, movements calling for the overthrow of the status quo include those that accused the grand caliphs, who were institutionalized as the Prophet's (PBUH) political successors, of straying from the purity of the Islamic message. Once the Islamic community became a great power, its stability rather than its orthodoxy became the guiding ethic, at least as far as the caliphate was concerned. So while the current call for social justice involves reinstatement of Islam as a universal system, that very system condemns the overthrow of stable governments, in the opinion of modern revolutionaries.[10] Still, the call for universal social justice does follow the spirit of Islam; and its emphasis in the modern milieu clearly fills the need for an effective and attractive sense of communal identity.

Secularism, Political Institutions, and Legitimacy of Power

There is another problem arising from reliance on archaic formulations of Islam, one with far more serious ramifications. The movements calling for the overthrow of unholy regimes and installation of Islamic ones define themselves as antisecularist: secularism is assumed to be a godless, amoral ideology. In an effort to resanctify the Islamic world, activists call for an end to secularism and reinstatement of governments whose legitimacy derives from divine sanction. As I have argued elsewhere, this is a misinterpretation of secularism, which is neither intrinsically atheistic nor antireligious.[11] It is a political form in which institutionalized religion remains outside the political structure in order to maintain its integrity and autonomy. More important, religiously legitimized governments are not suitable for today's geographically limited nation-states. Rather, they correspond to theoretically universal political entities.

Therefore, a potentially unlimited political mandate and the illegitimacy of protest or rebellion become the formal aspects of a political structure based on a religion claiming universal validity. But such a structure is an anachronism in today's world. The socioeconomic realities that fostered the rise of nationalism are no less potent today than they were in sixteenth- and seventeenth-century Europe. Economically autonomous geographic regions demand political autonomy; that is the reality out of which secularism developed. The era of its development was marked by almost continual warfare in which independent nation-states broke the economic and political bonds that kept them subservient to the central, religiously legitimized power. At the same time, they struggled to replace the universal Church as the community of highest allegiance. Historian Joseph Strayer describes this shift as one that "more than anything else marks the end of the Middle Ages and the beginning of the modern period."[12] In turn,. it made possible the development of political philosophy reflecting natural geographic limits of the extent of power. Even though the principles by which people were governed remained religiously sanctioned and were considered universally valid, the government itself was valid only for those by whose consent it was in power—generally an agglomeration based on cultural, linguistic, and geographic affinity. Secularism was an essential element in the eventual development of stable nation-states. Yet in the drive to resanctify Islamic politics, it has been obfuscated.

On the practical level, this has raised serious obstacles to national stability, as illustrated in the case of Libya.[13] Libya became a national entity in 1934, one comprised of Italy's conglomeration of three previously discrete regions: Tripolitania, Cyrenaica, and Fezzan. When the Allies finally granted independence in 1951, kingship was bestowed on the Sanusi leader whose ancestors' anticolonial campaigns gave him the only claim transcending regionalism. Yet Sanusi leadership and legitimacy remained a function of Islam, not Libyan nationalism. When Qadhdhafi came to power in the 1969 military coup, he set about gaining popular support. Naturally he chose the most effective vehicle: the only model in Libyan history—Islamic sentiment. He reinstated many elements of Islamic law, and 'Ulema were given positions of prominence in the administration.

Yet Qadhdhafi still craved independent authority, and he did not appreciate the 'Ulema's criticism of his reforms. In what can only be construed as an attempt to secure an independent basis of legitimacy, he eventually formulated his own ideology: the Third International Theory contained in the three volumes of *The Green Book*. There he specifically states that, while the theory is based on both religion and nationalism, it is "an international ideology, not a national movement."[14]

Qadhdhafi's meaning is that any national entity has the right to exist free of oppression and colonial domination. It has the right to establish its own political and religious identity. For that reason he supports what he considers just revolutionary movements around the world. Nevertheless, his own claims to Islamic purity are a form of religious legitimacy that other leaders in the Islamic world understandably consider threatening. For if Qadhdhafi's is true Islamic leadership, then, by implication, theirs is not. The colonel's operations in Egypt, the Sudan, and Chad are taken as convincing evidence of his expansionist plans.

Whether or not Qadhdhafi is capable of pursuing such goals further, his appeal to Islamic unity is clearly perceived as a potent force, particularly because there are few Arab leaders who do not have some kind of recourse to Islam.[15] While they do not necessarily derive their legitimacy solely from religious appeal, none can afford to ignore this force altogether. Qadhdhafi's overt appeal to Islam has therefore led to his virtual isolation among regional leaders. As Lisa Anderson concludes, "the importance of Islam in Libya also reflects . . . in its individual way the larger questions of political identity in the Muslim Arab world, where the *raison d'être* of the state remains unresolved."[16]

Ayatollah Khomeini's war against Iraq provides another example of the practical ramifications of religiously legitimized government in the nationalist context. While border disputes formed the proximate cause of the war, Khomeini's refusal to negotiate an end to the hostilities was only justified by Islamic purity. Nothing short of Saddam Hussein's overthrow—in the name of *Jihad* (holy war)—would satisfy the *Imam*'s (the religious leader's) demands. Even then, Khomeini vowed repeatedly that Baghdad is only a step on the journey to Jerusalem. This was no doubt a key issue in the growing rift between Iran and Syria at the end of the 1980s. Syria was happy to support Iran against its enemy, Iraq, but not at the expense of the hegemony Syria sought in Lebanon.

Like Colonel Qadhdhafi's, Khomeini's appeal to Islam as the call for universal social justice was very effective. Each leader was able to garner enormous popular support within his own nation and beyond, and each successfully manipulated that support in the face of overwhelming odds. Yet neither man was able to achieve his stated goal. The ability to provide social justice requires an effective administrative and bureaucratic mechanism. Its prerequisites—secure borders, stable governments, regional acceptance, and cooperation—all remain elusive for lack of realistic bases of national political legitimacy. The popular appeal of the call for social justice is indeed an appeal to the most basic elements of Islam, and its articulation in the modern age—strident, simple, eloquent—no doubt fills a glaring need for a renewed sense of communal solidarity. Nevertheless, its use as a basis of political legitimacy is not sufficient for the goals it seeks to achieve.

This does not mean that Islam has no place in the political process. Indeed, there are some people utterly devoted to Islamic goals who have also recognized the exigencies of national political legitimacy and have been able to formulate what I call Islamic secularism: a sociopolitical program that gives primacy to the requirements of national statecraft, but does so in the context of Islamic social goals. Among the New Left intellectuals, for instance, George Tarabishi represents a Socialist view that explicitly acknowledges the importance of both nationalism and religion:

> When asked about the content of our socialism, we replied: Our socialism is an Arab, nationalist one, not internationalist. And when we were asked about the difference between our socialism and communism, we answered: Our socialism acknowledges mind and matter. We understood spiritualism as an idealistic value for which we adolescents strove, and we understood our socialism as one which devoted itself to the whole people and not just the proletariat. We believed that class consciousness contradicts national consciousness and Arab unity.[17]

Islamic Secularism and Socialism

Tarabishi expresses the views of an earlier thinker, Bandali al Jawzi (1872–1943), author of the first Marxist interpretation of the origin of Islam. Although a Christian, Jawzi wrote from the context of Sultangalievism—a movement among Muslims under Soviet domination that placed nationalism ahead of the class struggle.[18] The Bolsheviks held that the class struggle was the primary focus of revolutionary activity. Only when the proletariat was liberated would a just and unified political system be established. Then individual states would be superseded by an international union. The Sultangalievists, on the contrary, believed that the nationalist struggle was of paramount importance. All those suffering under colonial rule qualified as proletariat regardless of their social or economic standing. Only when they had united and cast off the imperialist yoke would there be any point in addressing the class struggle.

Followers of the movement retained Marxist political economics but rejected atheism. In fact, Jawzi claimed that Islam is quintessentially suited to assist in this process—to "mediate socialism to the East."[19] According to him, Socialist ideals are truly Islamic, and, conversely, the Islamic call for social justice demands socialism. Therefore, encouraging Islam in colonized lands would not only enhance the solidarity necessary for fighting colonialism but also create a just society.

Jawzi did not believe that Islam is itself Socialist, a situation that would be anachronistic. Islam grew up at a time when ownership of property and particularly the means of production were not fundamental issues of social justice. But in today's world, he argued, the most effective way to implement Islamic principles is through socialism. Furthermore, Jawzi claimed that a truly Islamic society will transcend religious exclusivism. In his *Min Tarikh al Harakat al Fikriyyah fi al Islam* (History of Intellectual Movements in Islam), he holds up the Qaramati community of medieval Bahrain as the best example of true Islam in action. Not only was it Socialist and democratic, it also placed little emphasis on the outward practices of religion. Although religious rites were not prohibited, "the Qaramati, like the Bedouin on the one hand, and the Ismailis on the other, did not believe in religion or its outward practices.... [Their real] religion was the great social goal which they served and firmly believed in the need to realize."[20]

In the modern world, according to Jawzi, religious exclusivism is only another tool of class oppression. Were the Prophet (PBUH) to witness any of the nominally Muslim communities that maintain a capitalist system of oppressed working classes and religious exclusivity, he would not recognize them as Islamic. Only those systems that liberate all people, regardless of class or religious affiliation, can be truly Islamic. External religious conformity is utterly insignificant, for Islam is at heart a system of social justice demanding human equality and freedom in all aspects of life. The most effective arena of Islamic activity, then, is the independent Úmmah, which provides economic and religious freedom for all citizens. In turn, those free and equal people will maintain a strong, stable political entity.

Khalid Muhyi al Din, speaking in contemporary Egypt, takes this position further still.[21] He also claims that Islam is essentially Socialist. Muhyi al Din is a Marxist of sorts, but this does not mitigate his Islam. Like Jawzi and Tarabishi, he accepts dialectical materialism as a historic methodology but rejects internationalism and atheism. His conclusions follow from the conviction that God's creation was given to all people, not just a class of owners. When a single group takes control of the Earth's bounty at the expense of others, it is the latter's Islamic duty to challenge their authority. If the usurpers claim their authority on religious grounds, so much the worse for them. True Islam is ruled by consensus, he argues, not divine authority. Religious authority is not a civil matter; the two spheres should be kept separate, as they were in Islam until deviations were introduced by the Úmayyads. In this way, religious authority maintains its purity, neutrality, and authenticity. Political authority arises from the people—who are to be guided in their religious principles, of course, because Islam's role is to guide the conscience of the populace. In placing sovereignty on the popular will, however, Muhyi al Din articulates a theory of government whose principles are universal but whose reign extends only as far as the populace that legitimatizes it.

Among the discussions that followed the demise of the early modernists' popularity are often described as arguments for and against the caliphate. They center around questions such as, What will be the political structure of the Islamic world once the colonial powers are evicted? Must the ideal Islamic unity be political? If not, what role will Islam play? For obvious reasons there is a tendency to see the theories of Islamic secularists as a continuation of this controversy. I believe, however, that they represent an advance over the various versions of political theory put forward by the early modernists. Those ideas were formulated in a distinctly hypothetical context in which the possibility of a politically unified Islamic world remained a viable alternative. The Islamic secularists, by contrast, are dealing with autonomous national entities within the Islamic world as accepted reality. These scholars seem to reflect the recognition articulated by the Organization of African Unity in 1963 and the Congress of Non-aligned Countries in Cairo in 1964: despite the anomalies of their origins, the states that emerged from the ruins of the colonial empires are a fact of life. The most important item on the agenda of Muslim states, just as in all developing states, is to establish bases for their stability.

Antisecularist calls for the reestablishment of an Islamic state do not seem to consider this important recognition of stability. Granted, they are aimed at excising the sources of moral corruption and sociopolitical instability; they see Islam as the ultimate source of social and political strength and therefore seek to base political legitimacy on it. But they ignore the primary requirement of national stability: a source of social solidarity logically congruent with the nation's geographic borders. Religious solidarity cannot be thus contained; its leadership will inevitably engender national rivalries. Conversely, religious factionalism can hardly enhance the national stability essential for social justice. Advocates of a revived Islamic state may disapprove of secularism, although as Tarabishi, Jawzi and Muhyi al Din, among others, have demonstrated, there is nothing in secular nationalism that conflicts with Islamic sociomoral goals. Nevertheless, they may well have lessons to learn from these writers, at least on the issues of national politics and communal solidarity.

Notes

Portions of this chapter were published in Tamara Sonn, "Secularism and National Stability in Islam," *Arab Studies Quarterly* (Summer 1987): 284–305.

1. Tamara Sonn, "Recasting Islamic Modernism: In Search of Islamic Ethics," in *Studies in Islamic and Judaic Traditions,* edited by Wm. M. Brinner and Stephen D. Ricks (Atlanta: Scholars Press, 1989), 205–25.

2. The Quran uses the phrase *úmmatan wasata,* which literally means "median" or "mean" community. The phrase has been the subject of a great deal of discussion. Fazlur Rahman, for instance, interprets it to mean that Islam avoids

the extremes of both Judaism and Christianity. See his *Major Themes of the Quran* (Minneapolis: Bibliotheca Islamic, 1980), 45. In general, the phrase is translated as "the best community" or "the just community."

3. A. J. Arberry, trans., *The Koran Interpreted* (New York: Macmillan, 1955) 7:180. Compare 3:100, 106, 110; 9:72, 113; 22:42; 31:16; etc.

4. There were manuals of behavior but not in a category separate from religious sources or reasoning, as in the Christian world. The philosophical tradition of ethics adopted by the Christians originated in classical Greece, where ethics were a practical science and theology was a theoretical science. The two could be carried on independently of one other. In Islam this is not the case; ethical behavior is considered a response to the recognition of God.

5. Fazlur Rahman, *Islam and Modernity* (Chicago: University of Chicago Press, 1982), 32.

6. Editors' note: Dr. Sonn seems to mean here the jurisprudence parts of the Shari'ah. At the time of the death of Prophet Muhammad (PBUH), Islam was not the most dominant power in the world. By then the two most significant parts of the Shari'ah, the Quran and the Sunnah, were completed.

7. For a survey of discussions of justice in Islam, see Majid Khadduri, *The Islamic Conception of Justice* (Baltimore: Johns Hopkins University Press, 1984), 4–7.

8. From Ibn Manzur's *Lisan al Arab*, 13:458. Cited by Khadduri, *The Islamic Conception of Justice*, 7–8.

9. Edward W. Said, *After the Last Sky: Palestinian Lives* (New York: Pantheon, 1985), 34.

10. Incidentally, this is the context of the current popularity of Jihad as well. Perhaps in recognition of the negative status of revolution in Islamic law, the more religious term Jihad is often used. Yet its advocates involve themselves in a dilemma, as in the case of Anwar al Sadat's assassins. Like Khomeini, who perhaps was the most vocal proponent of Jihad, they recognize that their first task is to purify the Islamic world. Jihad's weakness is primarily due to its leaders, who are Muslim in name only. They claim Islam but do not fully implement Islamic law, thus proving their duplicity. They must, therefore, be removed. Islamic law is very precise about Jihad: it can be used only against non-Muslims and apostates—never against practicing Muslims. See Sonn, "Secularism and National Stability in Islam."

11. Tamara Sonn, *Between Qur'an and Crown: The Challenge of Political Legitimacy in the Arab World* (Boulder, Colo.: Westview Press, 1990).

12. Joseph Strayer, "The Historical Experience of Nation-Building in Europe," in *Nation Building*, edited by Karl W. Deutsch and William J. Foltz (New York: Atherton, 1963), 22.

13. For a discussion of the Libyan experience, see Lisa Anderson, "Religion and State in Libya: The Politics of Identity," *Annals of the American Academy of Political and Social Science* (January 1986): 61–72.

14. Ibid., 70.

15. See James P. Piscatori, *Islam in the Political Process* (Cambridge: Cambridge University Press, 1983), for a discussion of the role of Islam in legitimizing leadership in various states.

16. Anderson, "Religion and State in Libya," 72.

17. Cited by B. Tibi, ed., *Die Arabische Linke* (Frankfurt am Main: Europaeische Verlagsanstalt, 1969), 162.

18. For a discussion of Sultangalievism, see Alexander A. Bennigsen and S. Enders Wimbush, *Muslim National Communism in the Soviet Union* (Chicago: University of Chicago Press, 1979), 89–107.

19. For a discussion of Jawzi's thought, see Tamara Sonn, "Bandali al Jawzi's Min Tarikh al Harakat al Fikriyyah fi al Islam: The First Marxist Interpretation of Islam," *International Journal of Middle East Studies* 17 (1985): 89–107.

20. Bandali al Jawzi, *Min Tarikh al Harakat al Fikriyyah fi al Islam* (Jerusalem: Beit al Quds, 1928), 158.

21. The view expressed here is from Muhyi al Din's collection of essays, *al Din wa al Ishtirakiyya,* see Fouad Ajami, "In the Pharaoh's Shadow," in Piscatori, *Islam in the Political Process,* 19–22.

Chapter Six

Vicegerency and Gender Justice in Islam

Nimat Hafez Barazangi

In this chapter I focus on the Islamic principle of *al Khilafah* (vicegerency of human beings to Allah as the only God and the supreme guide), its social implications for the family, and where and how misrepresentations may have created gender injustice. Al Khilafah is the goal of the Islamic system: that is, it fulfills the purpose of creation and the will of Allah through human morality. I believe that al Khilafah is generally misunderstood by both Muslims and non-Muslims. The majority of Muslims practice it on an exposition level (i.e., a male political leader), not at the essential, intrinsic level of the principle (the *pontifex* uniting heaven and earth).[1] Furthermore, conception and practice of this principle usually fall outside the Islamic ontological view without considering the central concept of Islam—*Tawhid* (the oneness of God and humanity).

Unless scholars who are concerned with the study of the Islamic family recognize the different conceptual levels of the Islamic system, understand the variation in the implications of these conceptualizations, and use the central concept as their epistemological base, any attempt to understand or prescribe solutions for injustice in Muslim male-female relations will fail. Moreover, as long as Muslims practice al Khilafah on the exposition level only, they will fulfill neither the principle nor Tawhid. Tawhid, al Khilafah, and *'Adl* (justice) must be realized in action and change of perception. Such an approach to educating in Islam will change the present attitudes toward women's roles and achieve sociopolitical justice.

Tawhid

Tawhid means that Allah occupies the central position in every Muslim's thoughts and actions. "There is no God but Allah" simply means that God is perceived as the core of all values, the creator, the source of knowledge and the guide.[2] To perceive God in this way is not possible unless values are both perceived (hence known) and realized (that is, applied in real life). Therefore, God created one humanity to realize the imperative of creation, which means that His norms are for all humans (universalism) (Quran 33:72). By entrusting human beings with this divine will (the moral law), God appointed them as Khulafah (pl. of Khalifah) (Quran 2:30). This step was necessitated by a higher order of the moral action: freedom to fulfill or not to fulfill the will of Allah. To know the divine will, human beings are given two things: revelation—a direct disclosure of what God wants them to realize on earth (the law of nature, the system); and rational ability (sense, reason, initiation, and so on) necessary to discover the divine will unaided. For God's will is imbedded not only in causal nature, but also in human feelings and relations. Humans must exercise moral sense to discover His will. Once God's will is perceived, the desirability of its content is a fact of human conscience.

Moral action is not moral unless it is freely willed and completed by a free, informed agent. The concept of salvation has no equivalent in Islamic vocabulary. Humanity and the world, according to the stories of creation in the Quran, are either positively good or neutral but not evil. A human being begins his or her life with *Fitra* (natural endowment) "according to the pattern that Allah has made humankind," which is ethically sane and sound (Quran 30:30). Individual destiny is exactly what each person makes of it. If one relates Fitra to the most frequently recited verse in the Quran (1:1, *al Fatihah*, or the opening chapter, "In the Name of God, Most Gracious, Most Merciful"), the method of objectifying the Quranic principles becomes clear to the individual. That is, humankind is endowed with the natural perspective to understand the universe and act within the natural course of the *Nizam* (order). God's government is just (Quran 99:6–8), and its scale of justice has a perfect balance in the patterns of nature (6:115). This system of worldly and otherworldly rewards and punishments allocates for everyone exactly what he or she deserves (Quran 3:195).

Islam sees itself as relevant to all time and space, embracing all humankind. This totality comes from the realism of the will of God in all spheres of life. In its social dimension, Islam defines *al Din* (religion in the wide sense) as the business of life in space and time, the process of history, which in turn constitutes religion. "The religion before God is Islam" does not exclude nonadherents from God's justice (Quran 3:19). Rather, Islam in Arabic means acceptance of or feeling at peace with Allah's will as expressed in the different revelations. The processes of practicing Islam involve conscious piety and righteousness when well conducted (that is, following the steps prescribed by the system) and impiety and unrighteousness otherwise. Islam wants humans to pursue what is natural—to eat and drink; have lodging and comfort; enjoy sex, friendship, and all the good things of life—but to do them righteously: without lying, cheating, stealing, and exploiting; without injustice to self, others, nature, and history. Thus, the social order that is the natural objective of all humans is both natural and necessary to fulfill the will of God.

Islam calls humanity the "Khilafah of Allah" precisely because to live well is to fulfill the will of God and hence the purpose of the system. To facilitate the social order, Islam has introduced the concept of *Ùmmah* (universal community) within *Dar al Salam* (the house of peace) as the ultimate goal in time and space.[3] Al Faruqi (1986) believes that Islam offers the universal community as the basis of human association rather than the nation, the people, or an ethnic group. Thus, the Muslim political community is only a segment of the constituency of the Islamic state. Political and religious pluralism within the house of peace is possible as long as the will of God is realized and al Khilafah is understood and practiced within the framework of Tawhid. That is, the Ùmmah of Dar al Salam is the felicity of the social order (pluralism) in addition to *'Ibadat* (ritual acts) that also have a social order: "Proclaim the pilgrimage a duty to all. People will come [to perform it] on foot or riding from every corner of the world, that they may achieve benefits provided for them therein" (Quran 22:25, 26). It is important to note here that Islam does not separate the religious from political practices although in reality Muslims do. In addition, the usually claimed separation between church and state when secularism is invoked in Western societies is not a real separation because religious values still underlay institutional rules in these societies.[4]

Implications for Social Order

Only a small section of the teachings of Islam has to do with rites and strictly personal ethics. The social order is the heart of Islam; it has precedence over individual rights. Islam agrees with all the religions that cultivate personal values such as humility and kindness, but it believes those values are empty unless their cultivators effectively benefit others in society. The Muslim political community is guided by neither its own rules nor those of its people. Both are ruled by the divine *Minhaj* (system). The state does not legislate; it only executes the system. Thus, the ruler and the ruled are instrumental in the application of the divine system, whether in political or family affairs (Quran 3:104).

Tawhid and al Khilafah apply to family and male-female relations in three important ways: there is no particularism (i.e., unity of principle does not imply a unified practice, nor is it particular to some and not others), everything is relevant in time and space, and everyone must accept responsibility.

No Particularism

Identifying the divine will with value releases value from all entities usually recognized as its source: for example, sex, tribe, race, land, or culture. God alone is the creator, and every other being is a creature, all of whom are equally part of the creation. Hence, the belief in the unity of God implies that the same value falls equally upon all (Quran 2:44). This moral implication, however, is actualized by the free will of al Khalifah only if he or she fulfills the will of Allah. Therefore, any understanding or practice of value with a source that is not Allah causes injustice. In such a case, a human is stripped of his or her freedom to fulfill the will of Allah because he or she was made to accept a fellow creature as the source of value.

There are two basic principles in family relations:

1. Members of the Úmmah are equal in fulfilling the purpose of God; they have both religious and civil vicegerency (Quran 29:13).
2. The family is the basic unit of society; vicegerency starts with self and other members of the family (Quran 30:21).

Religious and civil vicegerency is partly realized by the most sublime act of worship—*Salat*—which also has psychological and social implications. According to the Quran (4:103), Salat is *Fardh 'Ayn* (obligatory for each individual). The Hadith says, "Five prayers are made obligatory by Allah Almighty, who ever washed properly and prayed at assigned times, and fulfilled their condition, s/he is promised to be forgiven, but whoever ignored (and did not do) them, s/he is not promised anything: Allah may decide to forgive or punish (narrated by Abu Dawud)."[5] The Muslim jurists are in consensus about Salat: it is obligatory for each sane individual who reaches puberty. Most Muslim scholars also consider *Salat al Jumu'a* (Friday assembly) to be Fardh 'Ayn. It is classified as *Wajib* (an obligatory act).

Individuals are rewarded when they fulfill their obligations and punished when they don't (Quran 62:9). The Prophet (PBUH) said, "Let those people who have left Friday prayers stop or Allah will close up on their hearts." *Ijma'* (consensus among *al Jumhur* [a community of jurors]) is that Friday prayer is Fardh 'Ayn because it replaces the *Dhur* (noon) prayer on that day and is required by the *Ayah* (Quranic verse) and the Hadith.[6] *Salat al Jama'a* (congregational prayer), particularly in the mosque, is rewarded more than individual prayer if it does not inflict hardship (an issue I discuss later in the chapter).

The Quran states: "*Salat* prohibits the works of shame and evil, the sinful acts" (29:45). The Quran also reminds believers of the pattern of human nature and needs (spiritual, material, and so on): "O ye who believe! When the call is proclaimed to worship on Friday hasten earnestly to the remembrance of God, and leave off business [of life]. And when the worship is finished, then may ye disperse through the land and seek of the bounty of God" (62:9–10). During the time of the Prophet Muhammad (PBUH), women conducted Salat in mosques: "Do not prevent women from the houses of God, and their houses are just as good a choice for them." Women also participated in Friday assemblies:[7] According to Um Hisham Bint Harithah Bin al Nu'man: I have not acquire (the Chapter 'q' and the Quran) except after the Prophet's reading it every Friday.[8] Yet many contemporary Muslims disregard these Ahadith (pl. of Hadith). Furthermore, the *Muqallidun* (imitators of precedence) often use them to urge that it is better for women to pray in their homes rather than recognize that these Ahadith are a license for those with hardship. Praying in mosques was practiced during the time of the early *Sahabah* (companions of the Prophet

[PBUH]). As Ibn 'Umar said, "permit women to attend mosques [at night]."⁹ Al Ghazzali used the same Hadith to support the argument that the Prophet (PBUH) permitted women to attend mosques.¹⁰

The books of *Fiqh* (jurisprudence) show consensus among the four schools (Hanafi, Shafi'i, Maliki, and Hanbali), who all agree that prayer is Fardh 'Ayn. As indicated earlier, according to the four schools, the first three conditions for conducting prayer are knowledge of the Prophet Muhammad's (PBUH) message, reaching puberty, and being sane.¹¹ Yet this same source adds, in a following section, a fourth condition, to Friday's obligatory status: the individual must be male. First, it suggests that the individual must be male but does not present any supporting evidence from the Quran or the Hadith. Second, the source adds that women are not obliged to perform Jumu'a; if they do, they do not have to pray the regular noon prayer. This ruling is contrary to the jurors' evidence that Jumu'a is Fardh 'Ayn. Third, it contradicts the ruling that concerns women's participation in the *'Id* (holiday) prayers. These prayers are enjoined on all Muslims and were highly recommended by the Prophet (PBUH): "According to Um 'Attiyah: the Prophet (PBUH) had ordered us to join the *Fitr* and *Adha* [the two holidays]."¹² Some schools of Fiqh consider these holiday prayers to be *Sunnah Múkkada* (confirmed acts of the Prophet [PBUH]), and others call them *Fardh Kifayah* (collective obligatory duty). If Muslim women are enjoined to participate in an 'Id congregation that is either Fardh Kifayah or Sunnah Múkkada, wouldn't it be better and more logical for them to attend Friday assembly, which is clearly ordered in the Quran for each believing individual and is ruled as Fardh 'Ayn?

In later years, Muslim scholars such as al Ghazzali (1058–1111) were concerned about the way that men were courting women and recommended that men should avoid unnecessary jealousy and women should be prevented from going to mosques. His judgment contradicts the Prophet's (PBUH) license that women could attend the mosque. Referring to the Hadith, Al Ghazzali added that "the correct action *now* is to prevent them [the women] except the elderly in order to avoid jealousy." He based his recommendation on 'Aisha's (the wife of the Prophet [PBUH]) comment during the era of Sahabah: "Had the Prophet known what women have done after him, he would have prevented them from going out [of their homes]." Al Ghazzali referenced 'Aisha's Hadith as *Muttafaq 'Alayh* (received general consensus), and added that al Bukhari had extrapolated that "the prophet would have prevented women from attending the mosques."[13]

The Muqallidun have since imitated and extended al Ghazzali's judgment, preventing women from attending the mosques by adding different levels of restrictions. Their reasoning has not regarded the relevancy of the context in which al Ghazzali made his recommendation (assuming that one accepts his rationale for the given point in history): they have knowingly or unknowingly forced particularism (i.e., a particular conception and a particular form of practice) on the meaning of vicegerency. By preventing women from Friday assembly, congregational prayer, and the mosque, they have limited women's participation in community affairs and the exchange of knowledge that is an important part of congregational prayer—both of which have a higher value than any of the reasons the Muqallidun give (such as to prevent *Fitna* [temptation or chaos]). They have also institutionalized an unwarranted differentiation between the religious duties of males and females. This differentiation has been unquestioned by contemporary Muslims, who generally consider it part of an Islamic ruling.[14] Thus, a dual injustice has been committed against women: they are prevented from attending a mosque, and their Wajib to attend Friday prayer has been revoked. Hence, Friday prayer is now considered a Wajib for mature, sane, free males only. Women are classified with slaves, boys, and the insane.[15]

Some Western and Westernized Muslim writers believe that, because women are banished from the mosque, their religious duties have been minimized to a few quick prayers at home. According to this view, then, banning women from public places reveals the discrimination inherent in Islamic teachings. Some of these writers reference the recommendations of al Ghazzali, the Faqihs, and other interpreters as well as contemporary practices and classifications of women. They conclude from these sources that Islamic teachings are to blame for women's oppression.[16] Although some writers do realize that the absence of women from the mosque has led to undocumented assumptions about the participation of women in Islamic life, this group is comprised of only few people.[17]

I believe that particular practices of certain expositions of Islam have replaced the underlying Quranic and prophetic principles. These practices have been transformed from temporal applications into principles themselves. I also believe that all parties who submit to such particularism commit an injustice by thought or action—including Muslim women themselves when they accept such practices without questioning them.

The Muqallidun who banish women from the mosque commit injustice on two levels. First, they make themselves legislators of a rule, using this verse to justify their actions: "O ye who believe! Obey God, and obey the apostle, and those charged with authority among you" (Quran 4:49).[18] Thus, they knowingly or unknowingly misinterpret both the central concept of Islam (oneness of God as the source of knowledge, value, and authority) and a basic principle of al Khilafah: no particularism in the free realization of the will of God. Second, although attending the mosques is only one aspect of the religious realization of the will of Allah, banishing women from mosques not only turns a practice into a principle but also violates the second principle of al Khilafah: everything is relevant in time and space. Furthermore, when human interpretation is given the same value and priority as the original principle, it violates another principle: that no human being may produce a rule for another human being. Only judgments that are relevant in time and space and that are drawn by consensus may be used for governing the community. In other words, any person, even *Wali al Amr* (a faqih, guardian, governor, or ruler) can commit injustice by changing a recommendation or judgment into a fixed law.

Contemporary modernists who do not accept the traditional interpretations of Quranic teachings usually assert that Islamic teachings themselves are unjust or obsolete and therefore Islam cannot be applied in modern times. They take certain practices as principles without investigating the original teachings in their holistic, historical context. Thus, these modernists have attached a value to mosque attendance itself, using it as a criterion to judge the religiosity of Muslim women and the credibility of Islamic teachings. By taking this approach, they may have caused more harm than good—and hence have committed injustice. First, like the Muqallidun, they attribute a value to mosque attendance that is different from statements in Quranic and prophetic teachings, where value only comes from Allah. Second, they have intentionally or unintentionally misled some women by making them believe that attending the mosques and participating in public life without constraint will allow women to regain their freedom of choice.

Lawal states that historic existentialism is known for its emphasis on choice and an attempt to define human liberty in a world that lacks values or a code of behavior. This humanist approach admits no criteria outside humans' awareness of existence as expressed through their own intellectual production.[19] By confusing humanist and Islamic meanings of choice, modernists have not only treated a symptom of a problem but have caused other problems to arise, the least of which is the reactionary measures of many Muqallidun. A worse problem is that few of the "liberated" women who have followed the modernists' views are able to understand Islamic teachings within Islam's ontological framework. Therefore, they cannot respond to the Muqallidun from the Islamic point of view. Many of these women still identify with Islam, and some have some credible arguments against injustice. Because they have not been trained in the science of Shari'ah, however, most view Islamic teachings and practices from a point outside the Islamic political praxis. The dialogue between these women and the Muqallidun remains a dialogue between mutes.

Finally, Muslim women often do injustice to both the will of Allah and themselves. First, they accept another's legislation as their source of value, hence violating the concept of Tawhid. Second, they do not exert themselves to learn and understand Allah's will from its primary sources. Therefore, they may commit injustice to themselves by not fulfilling the principle of informed morality and choice. One might argue that it is unrealistic to expect "oppressed, illiterate women" to fulfill the principle of informed morality—or any other principle, for that matter. But if illiteracy is the problem, why are most "educated" Muslim women (and men) deprived of a basic knowledge of Islam while still claiming adherence to it as their religion or way of life? Not knowing how to read and write is one reason for women's oppression. Nevertheless, some illiterate Muslims are more knowledgeable about certain aspects of Islam than many degree-bearing Muslims. Oppression may prevent a human from acting at the level of free will described in the Quran, but it does not stop her or him from thinking of ways to change the situation from within (Quran 13:11).

In summary, the battle over women's public participation is not helping Muslims understand Islam conceptually or systemically. Examples from recent history provide ample evidence that Muslims are drifting away from the basic message of Islam and immersing themselves into tribal, societal, and familial understandings of women's roles and modernism.[20] Fazlur Rahman (1979) distinguishes between the different movements within the complex phenomenon of Islamic resurgence, examining their views of the West, intellect, and Quranic and historical Islam. In his opinion, neo-revivalists perceive that Islam is related to everything in life, but their radical rejection of modernism has locked them into a position where they cannot either define goals or develop a methodology. As a result, they have selected certain issues to distinguish Islam from the West, such as rejecting bank interest, denying positive roles for women, and reinstituting Quranic *Hudud* (punishments).[21] The equation is missing rational scholars and women who move freely in all sectors of public life. More important, it lacks any understanding of the original principles in context and their underlying assumptions and ontological viewpoints.

The work of rational scholars and the participation of women in public life will help fulfill the will of Allah, just as the Muqallidun and the modernists are attempting to do if that is their *Niyya*. *Niyya* (human intention or purpose) in Islam is a prerequisite to any action before it is considered a fulfillment or unfulfillment of the will of Allah (Quran 2:225; 98:5). The Prophet also asserted: "The rewards of deeds depend upon the intentions and every person will get the reward according to what he [she] has intended."[22] Because intention should come from free will, it may be known only to the person involved and Allah. Thus, one cannot judge a principle as just or unjust simply by observing the practice of its representations. To understand if and when injustice to the Islamic system and Muslim women has been committed, one must clarify the perceived principle and then attempt to change this perception if it contradicts Quranic and prophetic teachings. Another criterion for recognizing injustice involves understanding the extent to which women's absence from the mosque has affected both their education and the role they have been assigned by a particular society. In other words, to alleviate injustice fully, we must first relinquish misconceptions about the principles and then achieve Islamic practices within the framework of Tawhid. Otherwise, symptoms such as oppression and illiteracy will reemerge depending on various groups' interpretations and their level of rationality.

Everything Is Relevant in Time and Space

This principle indicates that although there is no particularism in values, the application of value includes all goodness wherever it is found. This implies that society may establish a hierarchy of priorities. This principle also results in the flexibility of Islamic jurisprudence. There are five ethical classifications of human activities: obligatory, prohibited, recommended, recommended against, and optional. Any Islamic society may lose its claim to Islamicity if it restricts its activities to one of the five classes. The same is true if any Islamic society limits its practice of a certain value to the way it was practiced in a different time and place in history. Thus, totalism describes not only a society but a state administrative policy that assumes the application of al Khilafah.

This principle has two consequences for the Islamic family:

1. Vicegerency is fulfilled by all members' participation in both domestic and public affairs (Quran 9:71–72).
2. Vicegerency is fulfilled by guarding the two sectors of life (the domestic and the public) from immoral exposure (that is, from violating the will of God) (Quran 24:30–31).

Islam regards men and women as created for different but complementary biological and domestic functions. It does not, however, specify those functions or generalize them to other intellectual and social roles. "Do not enviously wish for that which God proffered on some and not on others. Men and women, to each belong the works they have personally accomplished" (Quran 4:32).

Two related Quranic verses have received great attention from both Muqallidun and modernists: 2:228 and 4:34. When considering the verse I just quoted (4:32), Muqallidun generally imply that verse 2:228, "the men and women having a degree of advantage vis-à-vis the other," often interpreted by many to mean "for men a degree over [women]," means that men have the advantage because of physical strength or financial expenditure. Hence, Muqallidun conclude that verse 4:34, "men have Qawamah (a responsibility) toward women by which God has bestowed upon them and by spending from their means," implies that men protect, maintain, and guard women because they support them with their means or strength. Fernea and Bezirgen explain how family and tribal customs prevailed after the early days of Islam, and why the basic premise remained that "men are in charge of women." Verse 4:34 is used in such cases to justify quite different practices with regard to women than what the Quranic teachings command and the Prophet (PBUH) had in mind.[23] Some Muqallidun have gone to the extreme, saying that because women are under men's protection in the domestic sphere, they are incapable of functioning alone in the public sphere. Thus, the home is their only place of function.[24]

The matter does not stand any scrutiny. First, it concerns only domestic relations. In fact, verse 2:228 concerns a particular relation during a divorce initiated by the male. The proof for my argument lies in the remainder of the verse, which concerns itself with the conditions of applying the first part. Interpreters usually omit the second half of the verse to allow for unwarranted generalization.

In a domestic relationship, men are at the head of households because patriarchy is the predominant form of family life, as most humans have shown since creation. The condition of the man must fulfill the basic principle of vicegerency (that is, informed and free application of the will of Allah) before fulfilling the principle that discusses mutual guardianship of the two sectors of life from immoral exposure. Therefore, if men demand from their female household what they themselves have not been able to fulfill (whether from ignorance of the teachings, because of tribal customs, or because they themselves are oppressed), it becomes injustice to require those females to be obliged religiously or ethically to abide by the instructions of their male household.

One might interpret this verse in the fashion of those who advocate inequality between males and females, including some Muqallidun (who advocate equity instead). Or one could interpret it in the fashion of those who advocate inequality in Islamic teachings (such as modernists who refuse any differentiation in male-female roles). But such interpretations run counter to the natural order of Islam, in which "the division between male Muslims and female Muslims does not exist—in thought and in principle."[25] These interpretations also contradict all the other verses that establish equality on the crucial levels of humane, religious, ethical, and civil life (Quran 22:41). The Quran asserts equality of males and females in the creation of a single soul (4:1), seeking knowledge (96:1–4), voting (60:12), receiving and dispensing of inheritance (4:7), and membership in the Islamic sisterhood and brotherhood with no distinction of sex, race, or color (49:10).

Role playing in a family cannot be considered discrimination against women. Nor does it call for segregation between religious and ethical obligations because both roles are equally subject to religious and ethical norms. Role differentiation, however, says nothing about overlapping activities. Where natural aptitudes make it desirable or necessity makes it expedient, men's and women's activities may cross into one another's realm without prejudice to the essential roles established by God in nature. Otherwise, the Quran would not have granted women full human, religious, ethical, and civil rights, such as creation of a single soul, inheritance, disposal of own property, voting, and so on.

As long as both scholars and practitioners view role differentiation as a problem rather than a symptom, the injustice that results from such practices may not be abated. As I said earlier in this chapter, placing practice on the same level as principle, perceiving one principle without considering the other, or viewing one sphere of life without viewing the other will always lead to an incomplete solution and hence unrealization of the divine will. As a result, one may be unjust to oneself and others, particularly if those discriminatory acts were purposeful and the agent was informed of their consequences.

Responsibility

The principle of *Taklif* (accountability) is necessary to keep totalism from becoming totalitarianism. Every human being, Islam tells us, is *Mukallaf* (charged with the realization of the divine will). Taklif is based on his or her natural endowment, which constitutes the *Sensus Communis* (what is shared with humanity.) This innate but educable sensus is the faculty through which the individual recognizes the creator and perceives Allah's will as the goal to seek in his or her life. This responsibility is the essence of morality. The Quran emphasizes the personal character of responsibility and denies every possibility for vicarious responsibility. Thus, it decrees that there shall be no coercion and requires *Niyya* for any moral act. There are three implications for the family:

1. Freedom of choice for all individuals to realize or violate the divine will; an internal decision to undertake an act and bear its consequences (Quran 39:41)
2. No coercion among family members in the perception of values; "let there be no compulsion in religion" (Quran 2:256)
3. No discrimination in teaching or learning value perception (Quran 90:8–10, 45:13, 43:10)

The Quran declares: "Nor can a bearer of burdens bear another's burden" (35:18). It also asserts that "Allah will never permit any of their good works to be lost, whether male or female." The latter verse concludes with "they [males and females] are members of one another" (Quran 3:195). In other words, men and women are mutually responsible for helping one another in their good work, be it guarding chastity, raising children, or even fighting.

Very rarely is a relationship perceived among verse 2:256 ("let there be no compulsion in religion"), its message for humans who accept Islamic ideology, and the meanings of the teachings of the above verses in one's daily life and thought. Verses 30:30 and 33:35–36 also are generally isolated from both this verse and the concept in verse 1:2. Verse 30:30, "So set thou they face steadily and truly to the faith: [establish] God's handiwork according to the pattern on which He had made humankind. No change [let there be] in the work [wrought] by God," is rarely thought of in connection with verse 33:35–36, "For Muslim men and Muslim women . . . has God prepared forgiveness and great reward." Moreover, both verses are hardly understood in relation to verse 1:2, "Praise be to Allah, the Guardian of the universe." The Arabic construct *rab al Usra* (the guardian of the family) refers to the male only as the guardian in his family's domestic affairs, not as the gatekeeper who controls female intellectual and social mobility. But such gatekeeping is widely practiced and propagated. In addition, female guardianship in her family is often ignored.

The Muqallidun's notion, extrapolated from al Ghazzali, suggests that a woman's chastity is the responsibility of her husband, her grown male children, and her paternal relatives.[26] Modernists believe that men, by claiming this responsibility, appoint themselves as decision makers for the women under their auspices. Therefore, this practice denies a woman's humanity and her ability to make her own decisions and bear the consequences. Modernists do not recognize that many of their concerns center on the loss of dignity consequent to the loss of power rather than the injustice or exploitation of women.[27]

Neither the Muqallidun nor the modernists do justice to women. On the one hand, the Muqallidun extend the male's domestic responsibility as prescribed in the Quran, making him instead the guardian of women's inherent freedom to realize or violate the divine system. On the other hand, modernists who appoint themselves liberators of Muslim women also appoint themselves protectors of women's rights. Furthermore, both groups use the representations of guarding chastity in separation from the other manifestations and away from the basic principle of mutual responsibility between a male and a female in aiding each other in the good work. As a result, both groups, particularly the Modernists have assigned a different value to the principle, thus, violating the central concept of Tawhid.

Implications for Religio-political Order

The religio-political order of al Khilafah is not limited to the elected or appointed leader: the caliph. It is realized by three principles; consensus of vision, consensus of power, and consensus of action. These principles, if understood and applied, can also facilitate the principles of social order.

Consensus of Vision

This principle implies that all humans are capable of knowing (1) the values in the divine will, (2) the movement in history produced by realizing these values, and (3) the present and how it can realize the previous two (the values and the movements in history) anew. Consensus of vision also implies equality in *Ijtihad* (self-exertion to know, understand, and realize values in present conditions). Ijtihad does not necessarily mean passing new rulings on certain issues when past rulings may still apply in time and space. Rather, it means exerting oneself to understand Allah's *Sunan* (the natural order of things) behind a particular principle and realize the multifaceted expositions of the Minhaj in time and space.[28] This realization will celebrate the diversity of interpretation. More important, it will internalize the diversity by applying al Minhaj to all avenues of life. Without such diversity, Islam will become an obsolete fixed law that can be easily rejected. Jawdat Said indicates the importance of Ijtihad in its widest sense—one that realizes the meaning of al Minhaj beyond the conceptions of systematic human research and methodology.[29] The Quranic Minhaj does not change; it was created on a certain pattern. What changes is humans' limited knowledge of its various aspects in time and space.

Consensus of Power

This principle implies that there should be equality in the social effort to move values from ought-to-be's into ought-to-do's. It also implies equality in the condition of al Nizam: everyone should be literate and literary in order to understand and follow the order of the Minhaj. This literacy does not necessarily mean that every individual Muslim has to be a scholar in order to be empowered (i.e., to fulfill al Khilafah). Rather, to be literate is to be informed of the teachings as a prerequisite of Taklif. Thus, an informed individual needs some basic knowledge and skills; without them, his or her share in the political affairs of the community may be reduced or diminished. If an individual who executes any exposition of the system does so routinely, he or she may not realize the social value of the system as intended in the principle. Thus, a woman who blindly obeys the orders of her household males or those of the Imams has not necessarily fulfilled her role as an accountable individual, one who is responsible for her action.

Consensus of Action

This principle implies equality in material and moral (educational) need. The minimum in educational need is what brings a full measure of self-realization as part of the Nizam. The ability to understand and share in political affairs empowers an individual to fulfill his or her role as Khilafah and, hence, become an active part of the Minhaj. Without this active role, the individual may not change history, which is part of the accountability involved in carrying the message of al Khilafah. To assume that only males carry this message is an act of injustice not only to females but also to Allah's Minhaj.

By applying these principles within Tawhid and in conjunction with the social-order principles, Muqallidun and modernists can deal with the issue of injustice on a level that makes mutual understanding possible. If they apply these religio-political principles within a particular governing body, role playing becomes temporal and may change as the system allows. Furthermore, by clarifying the underlying assumptions of different views and roles, individuals can realize mutual goals and work together toward eliminating their misconceptions and solving problems of injustice. An ideal of gender justice cannot be realized in Muslim male-female interaction without mutual trust, a change in attitudes about female roles, and a reexamination of contemporary ways of interpreting Islamic principles.

Notes

1. Seyyed Hossein Nasr, *The Need for a Sacred Science* (Albany: State University of New York Press, 1993), 103.

2. My basic ideas about Tawhid and its implications are drawn (and presented here nearly verbatim) from Isma'il Raji al Faruqi, *Tawhid: Its Implications for Thought and Life* (Wyncote, Penn.: International Institute of Islamic Thought, 1982). Nevertheless, the extrapolation and application to al Khilafah and gender justice are my own.

3. Isma'il Raji al Faruqi, "The Nation-State and Social Order in the Perspective of Islam," in *Trialogue of the Abrahamic Faiths,* edited by Isma'il Raji al Faruqi (Ann Arbor, Mich.: New Era, 1986), 47–59.

4. Eqbal Ahmad, "Islam and Politics," in *The Islamic Impact,* edited by Yvonne Y. Haddad, Byron Haines, and Ellison Findly (Syracuse: Syracuse University Press, 1984), 11–12.

5. *Al Fiqh 'Ala al Madhahib al Arba'h* (Cairo: Wazarat al-Awaqaf, 1967), 154–55.

6. Ibn Rushd, *Bidayat al Mujtahid* (Cairo: Maktabat al Kulliyat al Azhariyah, 1969), 159.

7. Muhamuad Bin Abdu Allah al Khatib al Tabrizi, *Mishkat al Masabih,* 3d ed., edited by by M. Nasir al Din al Albani (Damascus: al Maktab al Islami, 1961, vol. 1, Kitab al Salat, Hadith 1062), 334.

8. al Tabrizi, *Mishkat al Masabih,* Hadith 1409, (1961), 442.

9. Ibid., Hadiths 1059, 1082, 1084, (1961), 333, 339.

10. Abu Hamid al Ghazzali, *Ihya 'Ulum al Din* (Cairo: al Maktaba al Tijariyah, n.d.), 2:47.

11. *Al Fiqh 'Ala al Madhahib al Arba'h,* 151.

12. M. Naser al Din al Albani, *Hijab al Mara al Muslimah* (Beirut: al Maktab al Islami, 1982–83), 38.

13. Al Ghazzali, *Ihya 'Ulum al Din,* 2:47.

14. J. M. al Yasin et al., *Al Jadawil al Jami'ah fi al 'Ulum al Nafi'ah* (Kuwait: Dar al Dawah, 1987), 106.

15. Ibid.

16. Sally Green, "Reading Middle Eastern Women Writers," *American Book Review* (July–August 1989): 1.

17. E. W. Fernea, "Presidential Address, 1986," *Middle East Studies Association Bulletin* 21 (July 1987): 5.

18. For further discussion on the lack of a comprehensive, systematized approach in law and the Islamic social sciences, see Abdul Hamid A. Abu Sulayman, *The Islamic Theory of International Relations: New Directions for Islamic Methodology and Thought* (Herndon, Vir.: International Institute of Islamic Thought, 1987), 76–83.

19. Sarah N. Lawal, *Critics of Consciousness: The Existential Structures of Literature* (Cambridge, Mass.: Harvard University Press, 1968), vii.

20. Yvonne Y. Haddad, "Traditional Affirmations Concerning the Role of Women As Found In Contemporary Arab Islamic Literature," in *Women in*

Contemporary Muslim Societies, edited by Jane I. Smith (London: Associated University Press, 1980), 61–86.

21. Fazlur Rahman, "Islam: Challenges and Opportunities," in *Islam: Past Influence and Present Challenge,* edited by A. T. Welch and P. Cachia (Albany: State University of New York Press, 1979), 315–30.

22. *Sahih Al Bukhari,* vol.1, edited by Muhammad Muhsin Khan (Lahore, Pakistan: Kazi Publications, 1979), 1.

23. E. W. Fernea and B. Q. Bezirgan, *Middle Eastern Women Speak* (Austin: University of Texas Press, 1977), xxiii–xxiv.

24. "Jamaate Islami Circles in India and Pakistan," *Radiance Magazine* (3 May 1989).

25. E. W. Fernea, ed., *Women and the Family in the Middle East* (Austin: University of Texas Press, 1985), 216.

26. Al Ghazzali, *Ihya 'Ulum al Din,* 2:47.

27. P. Cachia, "The Assumptions and Aspirations of Egyptian Modernists," in Welch and Cachia, *Islam,* 210–35.

28. For further discussion of the different meanings of Sunnah or Sunan, see Nimat Hafez Barazangi, "Perceptions of the Islamic Belief System: The Muslims in North America" (Ph.D. diss., Cornell University, 1988).

29. Jawdat Said, *Iqrá Wa Rabbuk al Akram* (Damascus: Ayman Nwelati, 1988), 38–45.

Chapter Seven

The Nuclear Option and International Justice
Islamic Perspectives

Ali A. Mazrui

Two geographic partitions during the twentieth century profoundly affected the Muslim world. One was the 1947 partition of India, which gave the Muslim world the miracle of a new member. The other was the 1948 partition of Palestine, which gave the Muslim world the challenge of a new adversary. Islam in the twentieth century was never to be the same again.

The year 1948 was significant for Africa as well as the Muslim world, although initially the reasons were entirely different. In the year that the Middle East witnessed the triumph of Zionism as the Israeli flag was raised over Palestine, Africa witnessed the triumph of full-fledged apartheid as the National party was swept into power in South Africa. Only a prophet of biblical proportions could have foreseen that Zionism and apartheid would later become politically allied because of military collaboration between the two forces.

Where does the nuclear factor fit into this complex equation? The Muslims of South Asia have watched the nuclearization of their large, powerful neighbor, India. The Muslims of the Middle East have watched the nuclearization of their small but powerful neighbor, Israel. Over time many observers have wondered if India and Israel might conspire to prevent the nuclearization of Pakistan. In the Middle East, meanwhile, Israel alone has vetoed the nuclearization of Iraq and the rest of the Arab world while simultaneously facilitating the nuclearization of the apartheid regime in South Africa.

In short, the coming of the nuclear age has been bad news for both the Muslim world and Africa, at least for the time being. This has been compounded by the attitude of the United States, which has turned the other way and may have helped the nuclearization of Israel and South Africa. Yet the U.S. government has been strongly opposed to nuclear proliferation in both the Muslim world and Africa, taking this stance well before Saddam Hussein became the West's new bogeyman. On the nuclearization of India, the U.S. has been ambivalent. On the one hand, a nuclear India might reduce the arms race with Pakistan. On the other hand, it could counterbalance a nuclear China in the regional politics of Asia.

The nuclear shadow over the Muslim world probably began in the Middle East rather than South Asia. The partitions in 1947 and 1948 created military rivalry and technological competition in both Southern Asia and the Middle East. But technological change occurred much faster in Israel than in any other country in the two regions. Thus, the nuclear specter began in Israel, with consequences for not only the Muslim world but also Africa.

The Nuclearization of Zionism

In 1957 Israeli Prime Minister David Ben-Gurion proposed to his cabinet that a nuclear reactor be established at Dimona in the Negev Desert. Secretly the French government agreed (and may have offered) to help Israel design and build the reactor. In the same year a company was formed in Pennsylvania called the Nuclear Materials and Equipment Corporation (NUMEC). It was established by Dr. Zalman Shapiro, who had previously worked on nuclear research programs for the U.S. Navy. Dr. Shapiro was an ardent supporter of Israel. His company took on contracts from the federal government, including some that transformed highly enriched uranium into fuel for U.S. Navy reactors.

About seven years later the Atomic Energy Commission (AEC) discovered that at least two hundred pounds of highly enriched uranium were not accounted for at Dr. Shapiro's corporation. The AEC was also startled by NUMEC's cooperation with the state of Israel: the company was serving as "the technical consultant and training procurement agency for Israel in the United States."[1] Dr. Shapiro denied that he had diverted any enriched uranium to Israel, but he did pay 1.1 million dollars in fines for the missing nuclear materials.

Carl Duckett, deputy director for science and technology at the Central Intelligence Agency (CIA) from 1967 to 1976, later reported that by 1968 the agency believed that Israel had already developed nuclear weapons. The CIA noted that this development coincided in time with the disappearance of the enriched materials from Dr. Shapiro's company. When Duckett reported this information to his boss, CIA Director Richard Helmes, he was ordered to keep the findings secret. And when Helmes reported the information to President Lyndon Johnson, the president also preferred to keep it secret—even from secretary of state, Dean Rusk, and secretary of defense, Robert McNamara.

After France, then, the U.S. became Israel's second partner in the history of its nuclear development. At the time, France was an adversary of Muslim North Africa; and Israel and France had just emerged from the Suez fiasco of 1956. Their joint attack on Nasser's Egypt had apparently started out as a Franco-Israeli conspiracy, which was later joined by Great Britain under Anthony Eden. The United States was kept in the dark until the plans were ready. Those plans involved an Israeli invasion of the Sinai followed by a British and French invasion of Egypt, ostensibly to protect the Suez Canal.

Primarily because of American, Soviet, and U.N. opposition to the tripartite invasion of Egypt, the adventure failed in its aims. But the period involved substantial political intimacy between the French and Israeli governments, which was manifested in considerable anti-Arab and anti-Islamic sentiment in official French circles—an attitude influenced by Arab and Muslim support for the ongoing Algerian revolution. French-Israeli collaboration on Israel's nuclear reactor was partly an extension of their collaboration in the Suez adventure, but it was politically related to the Algerian war of liberation and Nasser's support for it.

It seems apparent that French collaboration was at the official governmental level. But what about American collaboration? How was the U.S. involved in the disappearance of enriched uranium from NUMEC? Was this collaboration purely unofficial, involving private sympathizers with Israel? Or did it implicate the government? There are a number of theories within U.S. intelligence circles and among commentators. Perhaps the most conspiratorial theory alleges actual CIA involvement in the disappearance of enriched materials and their diversion to Israel. According to this theory, Johnson was eager to cover up the issue partly because a major U.S. agency was involved. Another theory attributes the alleged diversion to Israel's own secret service, the MOSSAD, which subsequently worked out strategies for diverting both French and American uranium.

Basing his allegations on other evidence, Senator Robert Kennedy warned as early as 1965 that Israel had stockpiled "weapon-grade fissionable material" that could be used to "fabricate an atomic device within a few months." At the time, Kennedy's conclusion seemed very tentative. Nor was he aware of the cover up that was later attributed to President Johnson.

During the 1970s and early 1980s, the Republic of South Africa became the third country to feature prominently in Israel's nuclear history. Economic relations between Israel and South Africa began to improve before the October War of 1973, and trade between them dramatically improved from 1971 on. Israel's level of diplomatic representation in Pretoria had been lowered following the Sharpeville massacre of 1960, but it rose again in 1972 when Ambassador Michael Michaels was appointed to head the Israeli mission. In other words, the Israeli-South African axis was not born from black Africa's diplomatic break with Israel following the October War in the Middle East. It had already started before 1973.

Two areas of military relevance became important in the evolving collaboration between Israel and South Africa. One was counterinsurgency—techniques of combating guerrilla movements and terrorist tactics. Before the outbreak of the Palestinian *Intifadah* (resurgence) Israel was relatively successful in containing the operations of Palestine Liberation Organization (PLO) fighters. South Africa recognized Israel's triumph in this field and wanted to learn from Israel's expertise in counterinsurgency.

The other area of military collaboration was nuclear cooperation. During the 1970s and 80s, both countries were increasingly isolated internationally. South Africa had uranium and some expertise bequeathed by more than a decade of collaboration with the United States and other Western countries. Israel in turn had additional technological expertise that could enhance South Africa's military effectiveness. There is a widespread belief in both Africa and the Middle East that substantial progress in weapons development resulted from this collaboration between Israel and South Africa.

Suspicions about weapons development rose to a new level after the "mystery flash" that took place somewhere in the south Atlantic or

Indian Ocean. This flash was detected by a U.S. Vela spy satellite in September 1979, and its characteristics strongly resembled those associated with a nuclear explosion. The Carter administration kept the news secret for a few weeks, but eventually it leaked. Initial announcements attributed the flash to a South African device. But in February 1980 the U.S. television network CBS carried a report from its Israeli correspondent, Dan Raviv, who attributed the explosion to Israel.

Since then, alternative theories have been advanced about the mystery flash, including formal reports by investigative committees. They range from stories about a meteorite to South Africa's own theory that a small nuclear accident occurred on a Soviet vessel. Those governments eager to minimize the chances of a nuclear arms race in Africa or the Middle East must be tempted to opt for a scenario that does not portray either South Africa or Israel as nuclear powers. But the bulk of the available evidence supports the suspicion that on 22 September 1979 an unholy alliance between Zionism and apartheid was cemented, and the Muslim and black worlds will feel the reverberations for many years to come.

In 1990, on the eve of power-sharing negotiations with black South Africans, the republic's white government at last agreed to sign the Nuclear Weapons Nonproliferation Treaty (NPT)—making sure that what had been sauce for the white goose would not become sauce for the black gander. Before that time Egypt had also been persuaded or coopted into the NPT regime—but Israel still refused to sign.

Islam versus the Nuclear Age

Why has the nuclear age been such bad news for Islam? The new science arrived at a time when Islam was pushed to the periphery of technological civilization and the margins of scientific know-how. Gone were the days when Muslims were so advanced in mathematics that the very numbers of calculation bore the name "Arabic numerals." Gone were the days when Arabs pushed the frontiers of the metric principle. Who even remembers that words such as average, algebra, amalgam, admiral, alcohol, cipher, chemistry, and zenith were originally Arabic?

The arrival of the nuclear age in the twentieth century coincided with the disappearance of the Islamic caliphate, which had been part of the world system for centuries. The Ottoman Empire had disintegrated after World War I; and almost the entire Muslim world war came under

Euro-Christian domination—from Egypt to Indonesia, from Senegal to Malaya, from the Gulf states to Northern India. Never was the Muslim world more convincingly humbled. Ataturk's Turkey and Iran were barely independent. The rest of Islam was well and truly under Euro-Christian subjugation.

Although the world did not realize it at the time, two superpowers were about to establish a divided hegemony following World War II. One superpower was the United States—with a Jewish enclave that was destined to become one of the most important indirect factors in the history of the Middle East. The other superpower was the Soviet Union—with a Muslim enclave that seemed as unimportant in influencing Middle Eastern trends as the Jewish enclave in the United States was decisive.

By the 1980s the Soviet Union had a Muslim population of well over fifty million in a total population of two hundred and fifty million. The United States had a Jewish population of less than seven million in a total population of two hundred and twenty million. Yet the Jewish population of the Western superpower had more relevance for Islamic history than the nearly fifty million Muslims in the Soviet Union. One reason is simply the fact that the Soviet Union was not a liberal democracy; therefore, electoral numbers counted less than they did in the United States. Undoubtedly, fifty million Muslims in the United States would have changed the history of the world—for better or worse.

But of course this did not happen. The superpower that emerged as the nuclear leader in world politics was the one with a powerful Jewish enclave. Thus, the Islamic factor in the nuclear history of the world was doubly marginalized—not least because Western Jews were among the innovative giants of the nuclear age while Muslim scholars were scientifically peripheral in the twentieth century. The era of the atom was also the era of Albert Einstein, the most important scientist of the twentieth century and one of the most famous Jews of all time. The stage was set for a future Jewish involvement in the nuclear age (Einstein, Oppenheimer, Teller).

In a sense, we have come back to the issue of a nuclearized Jewish state. No collective reincarnation in history has been more dramatic than the re-creation of the Jewish state. The last Jewish state died two thousand years ago, only to be reborn in the full scientific glare of the nuclear age—within three years of the dropping of the atomic bombs on Hiroshima and Nagasaki. In a single generation the Jewish state itself became a nuclear power. Without this power, Israel's conventional superiority could one day have been neutralized by Arab numerical preponderance as the skill and organizational differential between Arabs and Israelis narrowed. But the acquisition of nuclear weapons has helped Israel create a potentially permanent military stalemate. Even when the Arabs one day equal the Israelis in conventional weapons and match them in nuclear capacity, the nuclear deterrent may work in the Arab-Israeli conflict with greater certainty than in the East-West conflict.

Israel happened to have been created at a time when a nuclear stalemate could conceivably ensure its survival. That may be good for world Jewry, but it is not necessarily good news for the Muslim world if Jerusalem is forever lost to Muslim sovereignty. The Cold War between East and West has now ended, and some conflicts between Israel and Palestine are in the process of being resolved. But if the U.S. and the Soviet Union nearly went to war over Cuba in 1962, will Israel and the Arabs still go to war over Jerusalem?

If we consider the peaceful uses for atomic energy, we can still argue that the nuclear age remains a disservice to Islam. Oil rather than uranium ore has given Islam new economic leverage in the world system. The Organization of Petroleum Exporting Countries (OPEC) is primarily a Muslim organization and is Arab-led. The Muslim world's margin of advantage is petroleum rather than uranium. While Muslim countries might themselves wish to learn nuclear technology and use nuclear power domestically, it is not in their interest that the rest of the world should substitute nuclear power over petroleum power.

The Crescent over the Mushroom Cloud

If Islam gets nuclearized before the end of the century, two regional rivalries will likely play an important part. One is the rivalry between India and Pakistan; the other is the rivalry between Israel and the Arabs. Saddam Hussein's aspirations in Iraq are part of a wider story of ambition and frustration.

India may have decided to speed up its nuclear program because of China, but Pakistan's decision to speed up its own program was almost certainly influenced by India's 1974 explosion of a nuclear device. The Indian government's attitude toward Pakistan has little to do with the fact that Pakistan is a Muslim country; India deals with a variety of other Muslim countries on an entirely different basis. But Pakistan's attitude toward India is often clouded by the historical rivalry between Muslims and Hindus. India is a secular state, while Pakistan is an Islamic republic. Thus, Pakistani perceptions of the state are conditioned by cultural and religious self-consciousness. Pursuing nuclear energy and achieving the status of belonging to the nuclear club inevitably carry a sense of Muslim pride and cultural ambition. There is a basic dialectic in the Pakistani psyche between Islam as a religion and Islam as the antithesis of Hinduism, which has conditioned Pakistan's nuclear program as it has conditioned its other national, regional, and global policies. The republic's nuclear ambitions go back to the late prime minister Zulkifar Ali Bhutto. For him and subsequent leaders, nuclear capability was part of cultural and religious vindication. Bhutto was quoted as saying, "There was a Christian bomb, a Jewish bomb, and now a Hindu bomb. Why not an Islamic bomb?"[2]

Pakistan's effort to match India's nuclear capability has been considerably aided by the work of Dr. Abdel Qader Khan. While working in a laboratory in Amsterdam, Dr. Khan gained access to a wide range of classified documents and scientific processes relevant to sensitive nuclear research. According to reports, he was even able to spend some time at the URENCO consortium's[3] secret uranium-enrichment plant at Almelo near the border of Germany and the Netherlands. Thus, he was able to observe the centrifuge process closely.

Apparently, Khan originally accepted the job in the Netherlands purely to make living en route to becoming a Dutch citizen. (He was partly educated in Holland and married to a Dutch woman.) Reports imply that in 1974—presumably after India's explosion of its nuclear device, which had an enormous impact on Pakistanis still reeling from defeat in the 1971 Indo-Pakistani War—Khan was apparently persuaded to become a nuclear spy for Pakistan. Later he left Holland to go back to his native country and became in absentia the most controversial Third World scientist in recent history. Holland was taken to task by its Urenco partners, Britain and West Germany; and the Israelis also lodged a vigorous protest. The United States temporarily suspended most forms of aid to Pakistan, and much of the world speculated whether Libyan money and Pakistani know-how were on their way toward nuclearizing Islam.

While Pakistan's nuclear ambitions have been conditioned by its rivalry with India, Libya's military ambitions are connected to its bid for leadership in the Arab world and hostility toward Israel. But Iraq has turned out to be a more likely nuclear innovator. International controversy erupted in the summer of 1980 concerning a French nuclear deal with the Iraqi government. According to reports, one hundred technicians from the French government company Technitome (an arm of France's atomic energy commission) were in Iraq to install a powerful Osiris resurge reactor and a smaller Isis reactor. The contract also included supplying enriched uranium, and the technicians were scheduled to train six hundred Iraqis to run the reactors. Voices of protest were soon heard, especially from Israel, Britain, and the United States.

Reportedly, the first shipment of approximately thirty-three pounds of highly enriched uranium (out of a total of some 158 pounds over three years) left for Iraq in June 1980. Western scientists calculated that 158 pounds of the 93-percent enriched uranium could enable Iraq to make between three and six nuclear bombs. Scientists estimated that it would take Iraq approximately five years to acquire this modest military nuclear capability.[4]

Early on, there was suspicion that the Israelis would attempt to abort the French-Iraqi deal, even to the extent of attempting murder and sabotage. Important parts of one reactor were blown up in 1979 in a commando-style operation, and an Egyptian nuclear expert working for Iraq was murdered in Paris in June 1979. French authorities and others strongly suspected Israeli involvement. During the summer of 1980, Western diplomats expressed fears about possible Israeli preemptive military action if intelligence revealed that Iraq was about to build nuclear weapons. As it turned out, Israel did not wait for such evidence before destroying Iraq's reactor in June 1981. Did Israeli aggression in Iraq inflate rather than reduce Iraq's military ambitions? Did Israel create a self-fulfilling prophecy—an Iraq newly converted to acquiring dangerous weapons? Israeli anxieties carry a certain historical irony. After all, France sold Israel a reactor without any inspection safeguards in the 1960s. While Iraq has signed the NPT, Israel still has not done so.

In the 1950s Israeli scientists at the Weizmann Institute reportedly perfected a new, economical way of making the heavy water that moderates the chain reaction in the nuclear reactor. Speculation has it that the Israelis sold their secrets to France in exchange for a reactor. That reactor, situated at the secret Dimona nuclear plant, was featured in a CIA report claiming that Israel may already have between ten and twenty nuclear weapons.[5]

Whatever may be the extent of Israel's nuclear capability, there is little doubt that the arms race in the Middle East, like the race between India and Pakistan, is a fundamental part of the nuclearization of Islam. Even peaceful uses of nuclear energy, the kind that President Nixon cautiously envisaged for Egypt, are only a few years away from potential military use, especially if political radicalism returns to Egypt.

How do these scenarios relate to global leadership and politics? The danger of nuclear war comes from two primary sources: vertical nuclear proliferation among the great powers and horizontal nuclear proliferation in the Third World. Vertical proliferation involves more sophistication and diversification of nuclear options and technology in the arsenals of the great powers, who can increase and diversify their destructive capabilities. Horizontal proliferation, on the other hand, involves entirely new members of the nuclear club. The NPT was intended to deal with the risk of both vertical and horizontal proliferation. The great powers were supposed to embark on effective steps toward disarmament while helping to reduce the risk that more countries would acquire nuclear weapons. In reality, however, both vertical and horizontal proliferation have increased; and the vertical variety has escalated faster than the horizontal.

What might effectively motivate the great powers not only to decelerate the arms race but also to declare nuclear weapons illegitimate and subsequently start the process of conventional disarmament? Vertical proliferation has sometimes motivated the great powers to seek ways of containing the arms race. For example, the Strategic Arms Limitation Treaties (SALT) were in part a response to the stresses of vertical nuclear proliferation—a search for ways of containing the competition. Yet for the time being, vertical nuclear proliferation has not been adequate for the bigger goal of motivating the great powers to give up nuclear weapons altogether.

What sort of concern is likely to be effective enough to lead to military denuclearization of the world? One shock might be a limited and accidental military nuclear catastrophe. The civilian accident at Three Mile Island in Pennsylvania did more for the antinuclear movement in the West than almost anything else before the Soviet accident at Chernobyl. Had the accident gotten out of hand and a bigger catastrophe resulted, the revulsion for nuclear energy would have been even more dramatic. Similarly, if periodic U.S. computer errors about a Soviet attack had resulted in a precipitate American response, the disaster might have created enough shock to propel an irresistible antinuclear movement among the populations of the great powers.

But one should not pray for disasters, however accidental. An alternative approach to shocking the world into nuclear renunciation is to take a risk with horizontal proliferation. In this scenario, the possibility—if not the certainty—of a disaster remains. The logic here is that a certain degree of nuclear proliferation in the world is bound to increase nuclear anxieties within the populations of the great powers and strengthen pressure for the total abandonment of nuclear weapons. The great powers do not trust Third World countries with those weapons. That distrust could become an asset if the threat of Third World nuclearization creates enough consternation in the Northern hemisphere to result in a massive international movement to declare nuclear weapons illegitimate for all and put an end to every nuclear arsenal. Thus, although the greatest risks of nuclear war come from vertical proliferation in the Northern hemisphere, the vertical variety alone has not been enough to end the danger. "Vaccinating" horizontal nuclear proliferation might be needed to cure the world of this malaise—in other words, a dose of the disease may be part of the necessary cure.

Here, the Muslim world becomes relevant again. As far as global war is concerned, the most dangerous part of the Third World is the Middle East. Modest horizontal proliferation in this region would be more dangerous in global terms than a slightly higher level of proliferation in, for example, Latin America or black Africa, partly because a regional war in the Middle East is more likely to escalate into a world war than a regional war in Latin America or black Africa. If horizontal nuclear proliferation is a necessary vaccine against the existing nuclear order, proliferation in the heart of the Muslim world should work faster than proliferation elsewhere. Although Brazil is much larger than either Iran or Iraq, its nuclear capability would be less of a global shock than Iranian or Iraqi nuclear bombs. Pakistan's explosion of a nuclear device would spark greater fears than a successful explosion in Argentina, and three nuclear powers in the Islamic world could be a greater threat to world peace than five nuclear powers in some other parts of the Third World. Thus, in the global struggle against nuclear weapons, the Muslim world might well play a decisive role in the future. At first, Islam might play Russian nuclear roulette with two other civilizations: Hinduism in Southern Asia and Zionism and politicized Judaism in the Middle East. But from this dangerous regional game might emerge an impetus for global reform—from limited horizontal proliferation might ultimately evolve global denuclearization.

Africa and the Traditions of Combat

The possibility of weapons of mass destruction in Africa has been explored in both the extreme northern part of the continent (particularly Libya) and the extreme south (particularly South Africa). For a while, Africa was ambivalent about militarism and rearmament, partly because of conceptions about the doctrine of nonalignment. As one African country after another became independent, each envisaged the task of moderating tensions among the great powers. The first conference of independent African states was held in Accra, Ghana, in April 1958. At that time the African states asked the great powers to discontinue the production of atomic and thermonuclear weapons and suspend all such tests "not only in the interests of world peace but as a symbol of . . . avowed devotion to the rights of man." The meeting reaffirmed the view that the reduction of conventional armament was "essential in the interests of international peace and security." The conference went on to condemn "the policy of using the sale of arms as a means of exerting pressure on Governments and interfering in the internal affairs of other countries."[6] Libya was represented at the Accra conference, but South Africa was not because it was still under a white apartheid government.

In those days nonaligned countries were still seduced by the ideals of disarmament, partly because of India's ambivalence about the precise relationship between nonviolence and nonalignment. The most important Indian contributions to African political thought were the doctrines of nonviolence and nonalignment. Gandhi contributed passive resistance to one school of African thought; Nehru contributed nonalignment to almost all African countries. As Uganda's Milton Obote said in his tribute to Nehru, "[he] will be remembered as the founder of nonalignment. . . . The new nations of the world owe him a debt of gratitude in this respect."[7]

But how related were the two doctrines? For India, Gandhi's nonviolence was a method of seeking freedom while Nehru's nonalignment was a method of seeking peace. In some ways, nonalignment translated into foreign policy some of the moral assumptions that underlay passive resistance in the domestic struggle for India's independence. Gandhi once said, "Free India can have no enemy. . . . For India to enter into the race for armament is to court suicide. . . . The world is looking for something new and unique from India. . . . With the loss of India to non-violence the last hope of the world will be gone."[8]

In spite of Gandhi's vision, independent India did not practice abstinence; and Gandhian nonviolence was not fully translated into foreign policy. Suspicion of Pakistan in particular was too strong to permit such an attitude. Yet of all the countries in the world and in spite of its wars with Pakistan, India under Nehru has come closest to symbolizing the search for peace. For a crucial decade in the history of Africa and Asia, India was the diplomatic leader of both continents. With its doctrine of nonalignment, the nation bequeathed to many new states a provisional foreign policy for the first experimental years of sovereign statehood. The wheel of global pacification had come full circle. Asia and Africa were colonized partly with the idea of "imposing peace" upon them. But now nonalignment had turned the tables on old concepts like *Pax Britannica*. Those who were once colonized were now preaching peace to their former imperial tutors.

Nevertheless, India's nonalignment was destined to go nuclear. Indeed, India was the first nonaligned country to explode a nuclear device, which it did in 1974. It was also the first country without a permanent seat in the U.N. Security Council to explode a nuclear device. The first five nuclear powers were also the warlords with veto power in the Security Council: the United States, the Soviet Union, Great Britain, France, and the People's Republic of China. India had broken this neat equation and placed the issue of nuclear proliferation on a new footing.

But is nuclear nonalignment a contradiction in itself? Should African states and other Third World countries continue to follow their tradition of distrusting militarism? If one of the ambitions of nonalignment continues to be an effort to moderate world tensions, then two Third World legacies had to go nuclear: the legacy of Nehru in India and the legacy of the warrior tradition in Africa. The nuclearization of nonalignment would mean not merely use nuclear power for peaceful purposes but to reduce the danger of East-West confrontation. The nuclearization of the warrior tradition, on the other hand, would imply a reassertion of adulthood in the Third World, a rejection of the imperial monopoly of warfare. Nonalignment would seek to reduce tensions; the warrior tradition would seek to reduce dependency.

India has already moved into the nuclear field. For the time being, it has assured the world that it will use its nuclear capacity for peaceful purposes. Nevertheless, it has warned that such a nonmilitary commitment partly depends upon Pakistan's nuclear policy in the years ahead. But how far is Africa from a comparable nuclear role? And in what way would proliferation of nuclear weapons in Africa be a contribution to global pacification?

Militarily, Africa is still a dependent continent in terms of weaponry. Apart from the white-dominated countries in the south—and, to some extent, apart from Egypt—the technology of making sophisticated weapons is a distant aspiration for African countries. But seven traditions of combat are particularly pertinent in Africa. One is the *Jihad* tradition—a commitment to defend Islam with the sword if need be. The second is passive resistance, which can be described as a Christo-Gandhian tradition. It combines a commitment to social transformation with renunciation of violence. Passive resistance often includes the crucifixion syndrome—the pursuit of martyrdom as a strategy of protest.

Curiously, the Iranian revolution's strategy against the shah was Christo-Gandhian in appearance but in fact derived from the Jihad tradition. Thousands of unarmed people poured into the streets of Tehran in what was the most impressive people's revolution of the second half of the twentieth century. It was also the most impressive case of passive resistance since Mahatma Gandhi inspired the masses of India to rebel against the British Raj. Thus, Ayatollah Khomeini was strikingly similar to Mohandas Gandhi in terms of their historic roles. Both leaders mobilized cultural and religious symbols to move the hearts of their compatriots against perceived injustice. Libya, after its 1969 revolution, included a Jihad factor in its foreign policy under Muammar Qadhdhafy.

The third tradition of combat is the warrior tradition. It survives in a variety of forms in different cultures—from the samurai code in Japan to the residual "deer hunter" image in the United States. The warrior tradition is based on the hard virtues of individual masculinity: toughness, courage, endurance, and ruthlessness. It survives in a variety of forms in Africa—sometimes disguised behind the uniform of a modern army.

The fourth combat culture is the guerrilla tradition. It has been particularly important in struggles for national liberation and social revolutions. Increasingly, this mode of combat has become androgynous, rallying both men and women to the struggle. The wars in Southern Africa belong to this category.

A fifth, closely related tradition is terrorism. It includes skyjacking, hostage holding, blowing up bars, and the like. But unlike a guerrilla movement, terrorism need not include an organized army, although it often requires operators and agents. Normal use of the term *terrorism* has been conditioned by the values that the power structure invests in law and order rather than fundamental social reform. Therefore, the word tends to have negative connotations. But my use here attempts to be neutral. Terrorism is a form of warfare rather than a form of deviancy. Just as there can be a just war and an unjust one, so there can be just and unjust terrorist movements. Like guerrilla movements, revolutionary terrorism now tries to be androgynous—recruiting both men and women.

On the whole, other forms of warfare destroy in order to incapacitate the enemy. Terrorism destroys in order to frighten the population. To incapacitate the war machine of the enemy is harder to accomplish than to erode the self-confidence of the population. Terrorism is often the ultimate weapon of the weak, a strategy of last resort. Lord Acton may have been right in his suspicion that "power corrupts, and absolute power corrupts absolutely."[9] Since then, however, we have come to recognize that powerlessness also corrupts—and absolute powerlessness can lead to acts of desperation. Terrorism is often born from the agonies of frustration. That is what the bombs in the markets of Jerusalem and the pubs of Ulster are all about.

We should also remember that the power structure of a state can also become terroristic. The record of the British forces in Northern Ireland has had its moments of moral degeneracy—as the European Commission on Human Rights has been compelled to note. But far more guilty of counterterrorism is the state of Israel, which has insisted on killing dozens of Arabs (no matter how innocent) for every Jew that has fallen in a terrorist act.

Marxist debaters have long agonized over the concept of state capitalism. Liberal debaters should also recognize state terrorism as an aberration with a logic of its own, even in liberal societies. The state of Israel is a classic case of a domestic liberal democracy that has produced a terrorist foreign policy. The periodic bombing of Lebanese villages has been a feature of this policy. The terrorist is not always the sly, disguised individual about to plant a bomb in a marketplace. He or she might be the ruthless state official who plans such acts and gives orders for them to be carried out under government auspices. Israel, for example, has plotted individual assassinations and kidnapping over the years.

But state terrorism can sometimes be an aspect of the sixth tradition of combat: conventional war—a confrontation between two organized armies representing different societies, states, or regions. This combat tradition tends to be de facto masculine, although not necessarily because of any conscious cultural logic. If the guerrilla is symbolized by the sten gun, the terrorist by the time bomb, the collective effort of conventional warfare is symbolized by the modern tank.

The seventh tradition of combat is what nuclear power is all about. Africa was in attendance at the birth of the nuclear age; Zaire's uranium helped set in motion the first nuclear reactor in North America. For better or worse, the continent's uranium facilitated those dreadful atomic bombs dropped on Hiroshima and Nagasaki in August 1945. Of course, Africa had no say in the matter. It was not an exercise in Africa's warrior tradition at all. An African resource had simply been pirated—and, like other African resources in the past, it played a major role in a significant shift in Western industrialism.

Toward the Nuclearization of Africa

Uranium was not particularly scarce, even in the 1940s. But outside the Soviet bloc and North America, uranium seemed to be substantially available only in black Africa. As Caryl P. Haskins said in 1946,

> [uranium] stands next to copper in abundance, is more abundant than zinc, and is about four times as plentiful as lead. . . . However, the outstanding deposits are narrowly distributed, being confined to the United States, Canada, the Belgian Congo, Czechoslovakia and possibly Russia. The fact that the richest deposits of uranium ore occur in a fairly limited number of places makes international control feasible; but it also foreshadows violent competitive struggles for ownership of the richest deposits (the struggle for oil greatly intensified).[10]

Since 1946, other reserves of uranium ore have been discovered, including several in different parts of Africa. African uranium has continued to fill many a reactor in the Western world and has helped to create many a nuclear device.

Africa rendered a second service to the nuclear age: it provided the desert for nuclear tests in the early 1960s. In this case, the continent's nuclear involvement shifted from a purely indigenous resource (uranium) to a partly Islamic context of sovereignty (the Sahara). Africa moved from providing raw material to furnishing a neo-Islamic laboratory in the desert for a Western bomb. North Africa was the first African soil to be violated by somebody else's nuclear tests—the French tests in Algeria before 1962.

Africa's third point of entry into the nuclear age was through the Republic of South Africa. Before the government of F. W. de Klerk, South Africa probably became a nuclear power—or was close to it. Thus, through indigenous resources, a semi-Islamic testing laboratory, and actual Western productive capability, a circle of influence developed.

The progress of the French nuclear program and its tests in the Sahara most likely helped Israel's nuclear program. During this period France was collaborating with Israel economically, diplomatically, militarily, and technologically. The French helped the Israelis build a nuclear reactor at Dimona and seemed at times to be closer to the Israelis than the Americans were. The cyclical nuclear equation was about to be completed: the Sahara aided France's nuclear program, France aided Israeli's nuclear design, and Israel aided South Africa's nuclear ambitions. Kwame Nkrumah's fear of a link between nuclear tests in the Sahara and racism in South Africa found astonishing vindication nearly two decades later.

In April 1960 Nkrumah addressed an international meeting in Accra:

Fellow Africans and friends: there are two threatening swords of Damocles hanging over the continent, and we must remove them. These are nuclear tests in the Sahara by the French Government and the apartheid policy of the Government of the Union of South Africa. It would be a great mistake to imagine that the achievement of political independence by certain areas in Africa will automatically mean the end of the struggle. It is merely the beginning of the struggle.[11]

Nkrumah's thesis was prophetic. Until the 1990s South Africa used nuclear power as a stabilizing factor in defense of apartheid, and nuclear fallout in the Sahara during the 1960s linked racism and nuclear weapons in ways that are only now beginning to reveal themselves.

Cultural and technological inequalities between whites and blacks in Southern Africa have affected other areas of security, both conventional and nuclear. In the past, South Africa has used its technological superiority to bully its black neighbors into submissive nonaggression pacts. Time and again, the sovereignty of Mozambique, Angola, Botswana, Swaziland, Lesotho, and even independent Zimbabwe have been violated, sometimes with utter impunity. European technological leadership over the last three centuries of world history has been inherited by people of European extraction operating in Africa, and it has been used as a decisive military resource against black Africans. South Africa's neighbors appreciate what it must feel like to be Israel's neighbor—for until recently both nations have seldom hesitated to use blatant military muscle at the expense of their neighbors' sovereignty.

Cultural and technological inequalities have also played a part in such politics of intervention. Israelis have enjoyed a long military pre-eminence not because they are Jews but because a large part of their population is Western and European. Had the country's population consisted overwhelmingly of Middle Eastern Jews, the Arabs would have won every single war. Numbers would have counted. Middle Eastern Jews in Israel are often particularly hawkish and eager to fight the Arabs, but their military confidence has come from European compatriots.

The danger in both the Middle East and Southern Africa lies in pushing the weak too far. We have witnessed how desperate conditions in each subregion can easily become fertile ground for varying forms of terrorism. In South Africa, political apartheid is coming to an end as governing power changes hands. But economic apartheid seems entrenched. The wealth of the country (from fertile land to lucrative gold and diamond mines) is still in white hands, while blacks tear each other's limbs in desperation and poverty. For the time being, terrorism has not gone nuclear. But if the cultural imbalances between Israeli and Arab or white and black deepen this sense of desperation, we cannot rule out the possibility that the weak might acquire nuclear devices from radical friends elsewhere. Powerlessness also corrupts—and absolute powerlessness can corrupt absolutely.

Should African countries stop thinking in terms of making the continent a nuclear-free zone? That position made sense at one time. President Nkrumah organized a "ban the bomb" international conference in Accra in the early the 1960s and considered an international march toward the Sahara to protest French nuclear tests in colonial Algeria. He froze French assets in Ghana as part of his strategy against the nuclear desecration of African soil, and Nigeria broke off diplomatic relations with France.

All this made sense at the time it was happening. But in the 1980s Libya under Qadhdhafy considered going nuclear and acquiring other weapons of mass destruction (although the West was ready to bomb any facilities). And what about Nigeria as a future nuclear power? Because it is Africa's largest country, Nigeria's participation is probably a precondition for transcending Africa's diplomatic marginality. Like its fellow giants—Brazil, China, and India—Nigeria should pursue the goal of a modest nuclear capability early in the twenty-first century. My own reasons for such a recommendation have nothing to do with making Nigeria militarily stronger. The ultimate purpose is making the world militarily safer.

In the long run, an alliance between the legacy of Islam and the traditions of Africa might contribute to beneficial equilibrium in world affairs. For Nigeria, Libya, and black-ruled Southern Africa, going nuclear would be a new initiation, an important rite of passage, a recovery of adulthood. No longer would the great powers be permitted to imply that such and such a weapon is not for Africans. The gap between the militarily powerful and the militarily weak will ultimately be narrowed by making the weak more powerful and then persuading the powerful to weaken themselves. African countries will not rise fast enough to catch up with even the middle-range northern countries, but they could rise sufficiently fast to create conditions for substantial global disarmament.

Toward the Future

For the time being, military disparities and cultural inequalities continue to condition the texture of world arrangements. In fact, during much of the twentieth century Marxism and Islam have been the two most revolutionary forces in the world. Outside Europe, Marxism continues to be a revolution of rising aspirations, while Islam is a revolution of wounded memory. Marxism is an ideology of how the lowly have risen; twentieth-century Islam is a lament for how the mighty have fallen. In spite of setbacks in Europe, Marxism searches for proletarian internationalism—a new order; but Islam searches for an old one. At best, Marxism is a cry for innovation; at its most obscurantist, Islam is a whimper for restoration and revivalism. Ideally, the driving force behind revolutionary Marxism is class struggle. The ideal driving force behind revolutionary Islam is the Jihad.

Between 1945 and 1985, Marxist (or Soviet) military power ran a close second to the First World power of the West. But Islamic military power during the same period receded to global marginality. Today, Marxism has become increasingly in favor of the global status quo. Former Soviet leaders became in effect leading apologists for the current state system. During much of the Cold War, their main criticism of the U.S. was that it has become a destabilizing force in the global equation, a threat to the military modus vivendi.

Islam remains the more frustrated force and thus is likely to take risks against the sanctity of the existing social order. In desperation, it may be forced to seek its own nuclearization. One possibility is to marry the financial resources of one part of the Muslim world with the scientific resources of another. Allah in His wisdom has made Egypt and Pakistan the scientific leaders of the Muslim world. Equally in His wisdom, Allah has made Saudi Arabia and other Gulf states the financial leaders of the Muslim world. A marriage of these two resources could narrow the gap between Third World Muslim countries and the privileged credentials of the capitalist Northern hemisphere.

Such action is quite different from the danger of pushing Islam beyond desperation to despair. The recent humiliation of Bosnia Herzegovina and the cruel Western abandonment of Bosnian Muslims is just the latest wound in the collective psyche of the Muslim *Ŭmmah* (universal community). Too many more may arouse the ultimate martyr complex, such as the Kerbala syndrome among Shi'ites who emulate the martyrdom of the Prophet's (PBUH) grandson, Hussein. Islam in despair could be pushed to nuclear terrorism as a version of the Jihad. Such terrorism—probably aimed against Western interests—may well be the outcome of Western and Israeli insensitivity to the fairness and justice inherent in Islamic civilization.

Can horizontal proliferation cure vertical proliferation? The West's racial prejudices and cultural distrust may well serve the positive function of dismantling nuclear arsenals around the world. But nuclear disarmament is not enough. We need to reduce the risk of war. After all, because the genie of nuclear know-how is already out of the bottle, it can be reused if war breaks out, thus inaugurating a new nuclear arms race. The ultimate evil is humankind's proclivity toward war, not merely the weapons they use to fight it. Islam and Africa will have to join forces in a search for a more viable world order. One day the warriors of Africa and the *Mujahidin* (fighters for Islamic justice) must put away their swords and spears and celebrate the liberation of Planet Earth from the specter of chemical weapons, nuclear war, and excesses of injustice in human affairs.

Notes

Author's note: This chapter is indebted to my previous work on issues of war and peace in the Third World.

1. See Peter Pry, *Israel's Nuclear Arsenal* (Boulder, Colo.: Westview Press, 1984), 28–29.

2. Cited by C. Smith and Shyam Bhatia, "How Dr. Khan Stole the Bomb for Islam," *Observer,* 9 December 1979.

3. In 1970, Britain, Germany, and the Netherlands had signed the "Treaty" of Almelo under which they established a commercial centrifuge enrichment consortium (URENCO). See, for example, Shrikant Paranjpe, *US Nonproliferation Policy in Action. South Asia* (London: Oriental University Press, 1987), 1.

4. A United Press International (UPI) report, datelined Paris, revealed some aspects of the French-Iraqi atomic deal. The report was carried by many newspapers, including the *Ann Arbor News,* 9 August 9 1980. See Mazrui, *Cultural Forces in World Politics* (London: Currey; Portsmouth, N.H.: Heinemann, 1990), 226.

5. Ibid.; Smith and Bhatia, "How Dr. Khan Stole the Bomb." Consult also Ryukichi Imai and Robert Press, *Nuclear Nonproliferation: Failures and Prospects,* a report of the International Consultative Group on Nuclear Energy (New York: Rockefeller Foundation; London: Royal Institute of International Affairs, 1980).

6. Consult the declaration of the First Conference of Independent African States, 15–22 April 1958, app. Colin Legum, *Pan-Africanism* (London: Pall Mall, 1962), app. 4, 147–48.

7. *Uganda Argus,* 29 May 1964.

8. *Harijan,* 14 October 1939.

9. Lord Acton, quoted in *Respectfully Quoted: A Dictionary of Quotations*

Requested from the Congressional Research Service, edited by Suzy Platt (Washington, D.C.: Library of Congress, 1989), 270.

10. Caryl P. Haskins, "Atomic Energy and American Foreign Policy," *Foreign Affairs* 24 (July 1946): 595–96. Consult also A. Boserup, L. Christensen, and O. Nathan, eds., *The Challenge of Nuclear Armaments* (Copenhagen: University of Copenhagen, Rhodos International Publishers, 1986).

11. Kwame Nkrumah, *I Speak of Freedom: A Statement of African Ideology* (London: Heinemann, 1961), 213. Consult also Ali A. Mazrui, ed., *The Africans: A Triple Heritage* (London: BBC Publications; Boston: Little, Brown, 1986), chap. 8; and Sadruddin Aga Khan, ed., *Nuclear War, Nuclear Proliferation and their Consequences* (Oxford: Clarendon, 1985).

Contributors

Charles Adams has recently retired from his position as professor of Islamic studies at McGill University's Institute of Islamic Studies in Montreal. The institute's director for twenty years, Dr. Adams principally studied Islam in the Indian subcontinent. His most important publication is *A Reader's Guide to the Great Religions* (two editions), and he edited with Annemarie Schimmel the *Encyclopedia of Religion*. Dr. Adams has been a visiting professor in numerous places. They include the universities of California, Alexandria, and Isfahn; the Institute of Isma'ili Studies in London; and the Ecole des Hautes Etudes in Paris.

Omar Afzal is a senior searcher at the Cornell University Library's department of South and Southeast Asian languages and linguistics. He has advanced training in Islamic studies and Arabic and is particularly recognized for his knowledge of Islamic *Hijri* calendar computation, Muslim family laws, contemporary Muslim history, and the local Muslim community of Ithaca, New York. Afzal is a contributing editor of *Message International* and the author of several books and articles in English, Urdu, and Hindi, including *The Life of Muhammad, Sources of Islamic Shari'ah,* and *Lunar Islamic Calendar*.

Mahmoud Ayoub is a professor of Islamic studies in Temple University's Department of Religion in Philadelphia. His well-known scholarly publications include *Redemptive Suffering in Islam* and *The Great Tiding,* two in a planned ten-volume series titled *The Qur'an and Its Interpret-*

ers, and *Beacons of Light.* He is also an adjunct professor at the Duncan Black Macdonald Center for the Study of Islam and Muslim-Christian Relations at Hartford Seminary in Hartford, Connecticut, and a research fellow at the Middle East Center at the University of Pennsylvania in Philadelphia.

Nimat Hafez Barazangi is a visiting fellow in the Women's Studies Program at Cornell University. She has published chapters and articles about education and development of identity among Muslims in North America, including chapters in Haddad's *The Muslims of America* and Waugh et al.'s *Muslim Family in North America* and articles on contemporary Muslim education in *The Oxford Encyclopedia of the Modern Islamic World* (1995). Currently, she is conducting research on the tension between ideals and practice in Muslim women's education. Dr. Barazangi recently lectured on this topic as a visiting fellow at the Oxford Centre for Islamic Studies, and as a Fulbright International Scholar for Syria she is conducting a serial research project during 1995–97.

Laurence Edwards is the Jewish university chaplain at Cornell University. He has directed the Hillel Foundation at Cornell since 1981. A graduate of the University of Chicago, he received his master's degree from Hebrew Union College in 1975, at which time he was also ordained. Rabbi Edwards has served as board cochair for Cornell's Center for Religion, Ethics, and Social Policy (CRESP). Currently, he serves as codirector and resource theologian at the Coolidge Colloquium in Cambridge, Massachusetts, an organization sponsored by the Association for Religion and Intellectual Life.

Byron Lee Haines received his Th.D. in Near Eastern languages and literature from Harvard University. He codirected the Office of Christian-Muslim Relations of the National Council of Churches of Christ, located at Hartford Seminary in Hartford, Connecticut. Rev. Dr. Haines died in 1990; but a book of his writings, *Concerning Means and Ends: Writings of Byron Lee Haines on Interfaith Relations,* was published in 1992. He also coedited *The Islamic Impact* with Yvonne Haddad and Ellison Findly.

Ali A. Mazrui is Albert Schweitzer Professor in the Humanities and director of the Institute of Global Cultural Studies at Binghamton University. He is also Albert Luthuli Professor-at-Large at the University of Jos in Nigeria and a senior scholar and Andrew D. White Professor-at-Large Emeritus at Cornell University. His more than twenty books include *Towards a Pax Africana, The Political Sociology of the English Language, Nationalism and New States in Africa, A World Federation of Cultures,* and *Cultural Forces in World Politics.* Dr. Mazrui's television work includes the widely discussed 1986 series *The Africans: A Triple Heritage* and a book by the same title that was a best seller in Britain. He has also published hundreds of articles in five continents and is involved in a number of U.N. projects on matters ranging from human rights to nuclear proliferation. He is the editor of volume 8 (*Africa since 1935*) of the *UNESCO General History of Africa* (1993).

Fazlur Rahman was a professor of Islamic thought in the Department of Near Eastern Languages and Civilizations at the University of Chicago. Dr. Rahman was an outstanding and distinguished interpreter of Islam in the West. His many scholarly publications include *Islam, Prophecy in Islam, Philosophy and Orthodoxy, Major Themes of the Qur'an,* and *Islam and Modernity,* all of which are widely read throughout the world. Dr. Rahman died in July 1988.

Tamara Sonn is associate professor of religious studies at the University of South Florida. She is the author of *Between Qur'an and Crown: The Challenge of Political Legitimacy in the Arab World* and the forthcoming *Bandali Jawzi and the Hermeneutics of Islamic Revival* as well as numerous chapters and articles on Islamic intellectual history. Currently, she is conducting research on Islam in South Africa.

M. Raquibuz Zaman is Charles A. Dana Professor and chairman of finance and international business at Ithaca College in Ithaca, New York. His publications have appeared in the *Journal of Economics and Finance, International Journal of Islamic and Arabic Studies, North American Review of Economics and Finance, New York Economic Review, Third World Review,* and others. He is the author of more than seventy-five journal articles; proceedings; and special volumes, books, consulting papers, and book reviews. Dr. Zaman has worked as a consultant to the World Bank, the Food and Agriculture Organization (FAO) of the U.N., and the Economic and Social Commission for Asia and the Pacific (ESCAP).

Index

Abraham, the Prophet, 32
Abu Bakr, 12, 24, 25
Abu Hanifa, 22, 23
'Adala (to make equal), 43. *See also* justice
'Adil, 19, 22, 43
'Adl, x, 19–22; as a basic attribute of God, 21; as a moral principle/character, 19–20, 23–24, 42–43, 67; as a primary principle of faith, 19–20, 25–26, 43, 77; as sharing (economic sense), 22, 26; equality of sexes to achieve it, 15, 23–24, 42, 44, 77; and law/legal issue, 22–24. *See also* 'Adala; justice; Qist
AEC (Atomic Energy Commission), 96
Africa/African, 6, 7, 74, 95–96, 98–99, 106–8, 110–13, 115
Ahl al Kitab (People of the Book), 17
'Aishah, 82
'Ali Bin Abi Talib, 25
Al Da'wah, 5, 43, 64, 67–68, 70–72
Al Din, 17, 73, 74, 79
Al Faruqi, Isma'il Raji, xi, 7, 16–17, 92
Al Faruqi, Lois Lamya/Ibsen, x-xi
Al Fatihah, 78, 90
Al Gharemin, 52, 63
Al Ghayb (Day of Judgment), 12, 14–15, 78
Al Ghazzali, Abu Hamid, 25, 81–83, 90
Al Insan (pl. al Nas), 12, 115. *See also* human being(s)
Al 'Irth, 4, 17–18, 48, 54–55, 88. *See also* justice

Al Khalifah/al Khilafah, 5, 6, 42, 77–84, 86–88, 90–92
Allah, 2, 5; concept in Islam, 5, 12, 77–82; consciousness of, 14, 64–65, 80, 83–84; law of nature/Sunan, 42, 43, 78, 91, 114; relation to humanity, 12–13, 22, 49–50, 59, 61, 78, 89, 92; revelation, 78–79, 89, 91, social order, 79–80, 91–92, 114. *See also* justice; Taqwa; Tawhid
Al Maslahah, 48, 50, 52–53, 61, 86–87
Al Mawardi, Ali Ibn Muhammad, 25
Almelo, Treaty of, 102
Al Minhaj (system), 77–80, 87–89, 91–92
Al Musharakah, 47, 54. *See also* 'Adl
Al Nasf/Al Nasafa, 19. *See also* equity
Al Nisaá (The Women, Surah), 55, 60, 84, 87–88
Arab(s)/Arabic, 20, 43, 66–67, 70–71, 74, 95, 97, 99, 100–2, 109, 112
Al Sadaqah, 4, 53–54, 59, 62
Al Salah/Al Salat, 4, 23, 80–84
Altruism, and justice, 33
Al Wasat; as middle course, 2, 65, 72, 74; as witness, in establishing evidence, 19, 20, 23
Al Zakah/Al Zakat/Tazkiyah, 4, 15, 23–24; institution of, 15, 47, 52–53; Zak al 'Ushr, 57–58
Androgynous, 108–9
Apartheid, 95–99, 106, 111–12
Awqaf (s. waqf), 16, 53–54, 62
Ayah (pl. Ayat). *See* Quranic verses

Index 121

Bait al Mal/central treasury, 4, 24, 54
Beatitudes, 33
Belief(s), 2, 3, 11–13, 18, 25, 29–34, 57, 66, 80, 98
Biblical, tradition, 27, 31

Caliphate, 67–68, 73, 77, 90, 99. *See also* al Khalifah
"Call, The." *See* al Da'wah
Christ, Jesus, 3, 20, 30, 32–36
Christians, ix, x, 3, 30–39, 72, 74, 99–100, 102, 108; dialogue, with Muslims, x, 41; interfaith discussion, 3, 30, 33, 36. *See also* justice
Christianity, ix, 3, 5, 12, 16–17, 38, 64–65
Charity. *See* al Sadaqah
CIA, 97–103
Congregational prayer. *See* Al Salah/Al Salat

Dar al Salam, 79
Decalogue, 3, 32
Dimona, 96, 103, 111

Endowment(s), religious, 6 16. *See also* Awqaf
Equality/equity, 2, 20; between sexes, 17, 65, 67, 87–88, 90–92; in inheritance, 17–18, 55–56; in wealth distribution, 50, 52, 55–58. *See also* 'Adala; justice
Exodus, 28, 32

Fair play, 2, 4, 15, 20, 22, 44, 48, 60–61, 65, 114. *See also* 'Adl; gender; Qist
Faith, 13, 15, 20, 22, 25, 26. *See also* Iman
Faqih (pl. Fuqaha, Faqihs), 5, 6, 42, 52, 81, 83–84
Fiqh, 5, 6, 81, 86
Fitnah, 6, 83
Fitrah, 78, 89
France/French, 6, 59, 96–98, 103, 107, 111, 113
Freedom, 4, 6, 34–35, 73, 78, 84, 89. *See also* Hurriyyah; Tahrir
Friday prayer. *See* Al Salah/Al Salat
Fuqara/Faqr (poor/poverty), 52, 55–60, 112
Furud (s. Fard), 49–50, 54, 60, 65, 80–82

Galatians, 30
Gender, 1, 77, 92; gender justice, 5–7, 42, 55–57, 65, 77, 79, 80, 82–83 (*see also* women). *See also* Al Nissaá, equality; fair play
God, The, 2–3, 5–6, 11–14, 16, 19–29, 35; God's authority/knowledge, 30, 31, 55–56, 85–87; covenant with, 14, 32, 33, 34; God is firm on justice, 19–21 (*see also* Qist); God's justice (*see also* Midat Hadin); God's mercy, 23–24 (*see also* Midat Harahamim); ultimate owner of wealth, 47–48. *See also* Allah
Great Britain/British, 6, 59, 97, 102–3, 107–9

Hadith (pl. Ahadith), 23, 25, 42, 43, 54, 56, 59, 61–62, 80–81
Hindu(s), 17, 102, 105
Hisba/Muhtasib, 51, 61
Human being(s), 2–3, 13–14, 21–22; central to Quranic teaching, 13, 78, 90–92; effort, 31; power of choice and knowledge, 14, 47, 78, 84, 86, 89, 91–92; rights of, 37
Hurriyyah/Tahrir, 42–43, 73

Ibn Malik, 61
Ibn Taymiya, 61
'Id, 54, 82
Identity, Islamic, development of, x, 1, 37, 41, 44, 47, 84; intellectual and spiritual, 6, 44, 66, 85; political, 67–68, 70, 85; Western, understanding of, x, 43, 44
'Idl, 22, 43, 67: *See also* inequality; Zulm
Ijma', 81, 90–92
Ijtihad, 91
Imam/Imama, 13, 25, 70–71, 92
Iman/Amana, 2, 13
India, 95–96, 100–2, 104, 106–8, 113
Inequality/inequity/injustice, x, 5–6, 11, 25, 39, 41, 47, 49, 50, 53, 84, 88–89, 92, 108–9, 112–13, 115
Inheritance, Law of. *See* al Irth
Interfaith, discussion/relationship, 3, 30, 35–36
Intifadah/resurgence/Nahdah, 43, 64, 85, 98
Iran/Iranian, x, 21, 26, 71, 100, 105, 108

Iraq, 7, 70–71, 95, 101–3, 105
Islam, ix, 8, 11–26; a central term/self identity, ix, 2, 12, 15–19, 23–26, 37–38, 67; "at peace, to be integral," 7, 13, 79; a pedagogical system, 20, 24, 26, 41–42, 77; economic system, 47–49; state religion, ix, 57, 71, 99, 101–2, 104, 113–15; "submission," 7, 13, 64
Islamic, ethics/morality, 5, 16, 42, 59, 65, 74, 86, 88, 114; ideals, 41–44, 56, 77, 83–84, 92; judges (*see* Qadis); law, 6, 38, 42, 65, 70, 75 (*see also* Shari'ah); judicial decisions, 4; reality/practice, 17, 41, 42, 44, 56, 58, 83–84, 86, 100, 102, 105, 111, 114; civilization, 41, 114; worldview. *See also* al Din
Israel, x, 6, 7, 95–99, 101–3, 109–11, 113–14
Israelite, 32

Jihad, 70, 75, 108, 114
Jewish law/teaching, 4, 27, 28, 32, 38, 39
Jews/Judaism, ix, x, 3–5, 12, 16–17, 27–28, 30, 35, 37–39, 41, 64–65, 74, 100, 102, 105, 112
Judgment, 15, 23, 33. *See also* al Ghayb, Mishpat
Jurisprudence, 5–6, 21. *See also* Fiqh
Justice, ix, 2, 8, 15, 19, 21, 27–39; as the character of God, 19, 21, 27, 31, 78; as a concept (in Judaism); 3, 27–28, 29, 38; as the essence of Islamic revelation, x, 2, 42, 72–73, 79, 114; as the law of the land (in Christianity), 3, 30, 31, 35–36; definite portion of the wealth, 12; economic, 4–5, 15–16, 22, 35–37, 47–50, 57, 60; in individual morality; choice, upright, character, initiative, 2, 4, 20, 22–23, 29, 35, 39, 42, 43, 47–48, 50, 66, 77–78, 91–92; in testimony; witness, 16, 19, 21–23, 36, 38, 43; international, 4, 6, 108, 115; political; the state, 2, 4, 19, 24–26, 35, 42, 77, 90–92, 109, 112; procedural, 4, 28, 29, 38, 42, 44, 67; public welfare, 2, 23–24, 33, 48, 50, 52–53, 61, 86–87, 89 (*see also* al Maslahah); secular conception of, 44, 57; social; in marriage 16–17, 21–22, 39, 42, 57, 59, 63, 67, 70–71, 79–80, 89–90, 92; to the enemy, 15; universal, 5, 25, 29, 44, 64, 68, 70–71, 113–14. *See also* 'Adl; al Wasat; equity; fair play; Qist; righteousness

Kaffarah, 54, 62
Khadijah, 17
Khalifah; Khalifat Allah; Khilafa. *See* al Khalifah/al Khilafah

Law, 19, 22; of hospitality, 54 (see also *al Diyafah*); of inheritance 2–6, 27–30, 36, 38–39 (*see also* al 'Irth); of knowledge, role of, 21; of the land (*see* justice; as the Law of the land); of Mutual Aid, 32, 34 (*see also* al Musa'adah); of nature, 32–33, 36 (*see also* Allah); of sharing (*see* al Musharakah)
Levy, to purify wealth. *See* al Zakah
Lex Talionis, 28
Libya, 7, 69, 102, 106, 108, 113
Luther, Martin, 31

Mahdi (Massiah, Redemption), 25, 26, 35
Makkah (Mecca), 2, 11, 12, 15
Malaysia, 4, 56–57, 59–60, 63, 100
Marx/Marxism, 7, 16, 72–73, 109, 113–14
Micah, 32
Midat Hadin/Midat Harahamim, 3, 27
Middle East, 95–96, 98–100, 104–5, 112
Midrash, 27
Mishpat, 3, 28, 29
Modern/Modernists/Modernity, ix, x, 6, 29, 54, 65–66, 68–69, 71–74, 84–85, 87–88, 90, 92
Moses, the Prophet, 27, 39
Muhammad, the Prophet (BPUH), ix, 2, 11–12, 17, 21, 24, 49–50, 54, 56, 59, 64, 68, 73, 81–82, 84, 86–87, 114
Mukallaf/Taklif, 89, 91
Muqallidun/Taqlid, 6, 43, 66, 81, 83–84, 87–88, 90, 92
Muslims, ix, 5, 15–19, 21, 24–26, 30, 35, 37–39, 41–44, 48, 50, 52–54, 57, 64–68, 72, 74, 95–97, 99–102, 105, 114
Mu'tazilites, 2, 20, 21
Nationalism, 29, 68–72, 74, 76

Nawayah (s. niyyah) intentions, 43, 86, 89
Nigeria, 7, 113
Nisab, 52–53, 62
Nizam (natural order), 78, 88, 80–92
Noachid, Laws of, 3, 28
NPT (Nuclear Non-Polefiration Treaty), 99, 103–4, 115
Nuclear; capabilities, technical, 6, 44, 95–108, 110–14; option and justice, 6, 95–115; proliferation, 4, 7, 104
NUMEC (Nuclearn Materials and Equipment Corporation), 96–97

Occupations, entrepreneurship; entreprenurial principles, 48–49, 51
Oppression. *See* Zulm
Orphan(s), 42, 55

Pakistan, 4, 7, 56, 58–60, 63, 95–96, 101–2, 104–5, 107–8, 114
Palestine/Palestinian, 67, 95, 98, 101
Particularlism, 80, 82, 84, 86
Paul, the apostle, 3, 30, 33–36
Pluralism/pluralistic, 38, 79, 91; and Christianity, 30, 37; and Jewish community, 29; multifaith, Islam, 17, 42
Polytheism (idol worship), 11, 12
Prophet Muhammad. *See* Muhammad, the Prophet
Punishment: and reward, 4, 39, 78, 81, 85–86; and suffering, 33, 39

Qadi (pl. Qudat, Qadis), 4, 22, 38, 43
Qist (upright, no injuries), 2, 15, 17, 19, 21–22, 29, 36–37, 39, 50; God as a witness of (shahid), 21; God established a fair world, 19, 20–22, 25, 79; in Mizan, 22, 50
Quran/Quranic, 2, 13, 18, 42–43, 47–48, 50, 52, 53, 55, 59, 60–63, 65–67, 74–75, 78–91; egalitatian teachings, x, 16–17, 20, 22–23, 35, 65, 87, 89, 91; translation, 7, 12; verses, 2, 7, 11–15, 21, 42–43, 47–48, 50–53, 55, 59–63, 78–84, 87, 89

Rabbinic, 27, 29, 38
Rahma, 27, 31. *See also* God's mercy
Rahman, Fazlur, ix, x, 2, 7, 11, 65, 74–75, 85
Relevance in time and space, 80, 83–84, 86

Religious leader/leadership, 25. *See also* Imam/Imama
Riba, 48, 51–52, 58, 60–61, 85
Righteous/righteousness, 3, 28, 29, 30–33, 64, 79–90; and inwardness/commitment/redemption, 4, 32, 34, 35, 39, 54; as Salih/Salah, 23, 42; God's, 36, 37. *See also* 'Adl; Tsedeq

Sahabah, 81–82
Sahara, 111, 113
Salama 7, 13. *See also* Islam
SALT (Strategic Arms Limitation Treaties), 104
Salvation, 4, 64–65, 67, 78
Saudi Arabia, 4–5, 56, 59–60, 63, 114
Scripture(s), Christian, 3, 25, 30, 32, 35
Secular/secularism, ix, 4, 5, 6, 35, 38–39, 44, 57, 68–69, 71, 74–75, 79
Shadhid, 21–24, 36, 38, 43. *See also* justice; witness
Shari'ah, 5, 6, 35, 38, 41–42, 52, 56–58, 60, 66, 85
Shi'ism/Shi'ites, 2, 20–21, 25–26, 114
Shura, 25, 89, 90, 92
Sin, committing of, and justice, 3, 34, 35, 39
Slaves/slavery, 11, 30–31, 33, 52, 83
South Africa, 6, 7, 95–96, 98, 106, 109, 111–12
State, the; alligance to; legitimacy, 36, 68–70, 75; custodian of natural resources/taxes, 47–48, 50–51, 56–57, 59; role in justice, 42, 50, 56–58, 79, 87; treasury (*see* Bait al Mal)
Sultangallevism, 72, 76
Sunnah (pl. Sunan), 17, 43, 59, 60, 82

Tahrir, 43, 84, 106, 115
Talmud/Talmudic, 28, 35
Tanwin (diacritics), 7, 43
Taqwa, God Consciousness, 2, 13, 14, 15, 23; ability to balance limits, 42, 85, 87–88
Tawhid, 5, 42, 77–80, 84–86, 90, 92
Testament, New and Old, 30, 32, 35
Torah, 3, 27, 28, 29, 39
Totality/Totalism, 79, 87, 89
Tsedeq, 3, 28–29

Uganda, 106
'Ulema, 59, 66, 70
'Umar Bin Al Khattab, 25

Umayyads, 67, 73
Ummah/ummah, 5, 73–74, 79, 114
United Nations Declaration of Human Rights, 37
URENCO (Commercial Centrifuge Enrichment Consortium), 102
United States, 6, 29–30, 38–39, 59, 96–104, 107–8, 110–14
'Uthman Bin 'Affan, 24, 62

Wajib, 81, 83
Wali al 'Amr, 84, 90, 92
West, the, ix, x, 1, 2, 5, 29, 42, 44, 53, 66–67, 85, 96, 100, 104, 107, 113–14
Western/Westerners/Westernized, ix, x, 39, 48, 65–66; Western powers, 6, 44, 98, 100, 103, 110–12, 114; Western secular states, 4, 5, 43, 79, 83
Women, 6, 16–18, 82–90. *See also* al Nisaá, Surah; gender; fair play; justice

Ya'dil (make equal among non-equals), 43
Yosher/Yoshrei Lev, 29

Zaire, 110
Zionism, 29, 95–96, 99, 105
Zoroastrian, 17
Zulm (opposite of 'Adl), 22, 25, 41, 70, 72, 83, 85–86, 88, 108–9, 115

www.ingramcontent.com/pod-product-compliance
Lightning Source LLC
Chambersburg PA
CBHW032301150426
43195CB00008BA/532